ASSESSING DEMOCRACY ASSISTANCE:

THE CASE OF ROMANIA

THOMAS CAROTHERS

A CARNEGIE ENDOWMENT BOOK

Assessing Democracy Assistance: The Case of Romania
may be ordered from Carnegie's distributor,
The Brookings Institution, Department 029,
Washington, DC 20042-0029, USA.
Tel. (202) 797-6258. Fax (202) 797-6004.

Design by Paddy McLaughlin, Concepts & Design
Cover photo: Agence France Presse
Printed by Automated Graphic Systems

Library of Congress Cataloging-in-Publication Data
Thomas Carothers, 1956
Assessing democracy assistance : the case of Romania / Thomas Carothers
ISBN: 0-87003-102-3
160 pp.   cm.
1. Democracy—Romania.   2. Technical assistance, American—Romania
3. Romania—Politics and government—1989-   I. Title.
JN9636.C35 1996
320.9498'09'049—dc20   95-50999
                                                                          CIP
                                                                          r96

CONTENTS

FOREWORD

I n America, it's hard to go wrong selling democracy abroad, even to a cost-conscious Congress and a domestically oriented public. Express skepticism or say a bad word about democracy promotion and you're practically, well, un-American. Propounding the virtues of democracy makes us feel good and it's relatively cheap besides. Conventional wisdom has it that if American democracy is the worst system of government except for all the others, the way we carry out our democracy assistance programs must be the best possible way to go about democracy-building, too.

Strengthening democratic institutions and processes has become one of the four core priorities of U.S. foreign assistance and a major feature of U.S. foreign policy in the post-Cold War era. Some three hundred million plus dollars are being spent annually on democracy promotion programs. However, there has been little real effort to determine what the effects of such assistance actually are, how it is perceived by recipients, or whether the United States is pursuing democracy promotion effectively.

In this penetrating analysis—the first of its kind—Carnegie Senior Associate Thomas Carothers takes a long, hard, detailed look at our democracy-building efforts in Romania—a fascinating "gray area" case. Though Romania has received considerable U.S. and European democracy assistance since the collapse of the Ceauşescu regime, political reform there arguably seems to be more posturing than process. Building on his past participation in democracy assistance programs in Romania, extensive in-country interviews over the past year, and his wide experience with such assistance in many other parts of the world, Carothers assesses the kinds of democracy assistance provided to Romania. He examines how such assistance relates to our overall policy objectives in the country and region, the impact it has had on seven institutions and processes critical to Romanian democracy, and its effectiveness compared to that of European donors.

The picture Carothers presents is mixed. He shows how the effects of democracy assistance have been less than expected and often negligible. He finds some of the strategies followed by the United States counter-productive—in particular the partisan approach of siding with some political parties over others. Carothers also highlights a range of positive effects of democracy assistance that tend to be underreported. He systematically evaluates the ways U.S. assistance programs are implemented, finding that in many instances they do little to promote—and sometimes even retard—longer-term democratic development, and he recommends alternative strategies and methods of implementation. Finally, he draws broader conclusions from the Romania case and makes constructive suggestions as to how our approach to democracy assistance can be improved in general.

Carothers's study goes beyond the lofty rhetoric and the reductionist methods commonly used to justify democracy assistance programs when budgets come up for annual review. His judicious criticisms do nothing to shake the general belief—one he shares—that the United States should actively promote democracy in the world. If anything, Carothers gives advocates of democracy assistance an analytical framework and empirical basis with which to support their convictions. But Carothers also makes a strong case that we must become more serious, more self-critical, less prone to fall back on rhetoric, and more willing to work with local organizations than with American intermediaries. We can do a better job of assisting than we have done until now.

Carothers's paradoxical conclusion: "The case for democracy assistance may at times depend less on the specific impact of the assistance on others than on what the assistance says and means about ourselves."

The views expressed and conclusions reached in this study are, of course, the author's own.

Morton I. Abramowitz, *President*
Carnegie Endowment for International Peace

ASSESSING
DEMOCRACY
ASSISTANCE

CHAPTER 1

INTRODUCTION

Since the early 1980s, promoting democracy abroad—a preoccupation of American foreign policy off and on throughout this century—has enjoyed a resurgence of attention from U.S. policy-makers. The resurgence began when President Reagan embraced democracy promotion as a major rhetorical, and sometimes substantive, theme of his foreign policy. He did so initially to give a positive, moral shape to his ardent anti-communist orientation, and later as a response to the growing trend toward democracy in various parts of the world.[1] The resurgence has flourished since the end of the Cold War. Both the Bush and Clinton administrations have stressed the idea that democracy promotion uniquely fuses America's moral and pragmatic interests abroad and is therefore the logical successor to anti-communism as the organizing principle of post-Cold War U.S. foreign policy. Although in practice the place of democracy promotion in the actual Bush and Clinton policies has not matched this rhetorical emphasis, both administrations have pursued democracy promotion as one of the three main elements of U.S. policy, alongside economic and security concerns.[2]

The tools available to U.S. policy-makers seeking to promote democracy abroad range from mild moral suasion to outright military force. In the middle of that range lie assistance programs that aim to support democratic development—including programs to reform judiciaries, draft constitutions, strengthen parliaments, fortify local government, build human rights organizations, support independent media, monitor elections, modify civil-military relations, bolster unions, and improve civic education. Such assistance has been increasingly pursued by the U.S. government since the early 1980s, in close parallel with the overall growth of democracy promotion as a general U.S. policy goal. In the early and mid-1980s, the U.S. Agency for International Development (USAID) and the U.S. Information Agency (USIA) began to develop democracy-related assistance programs, particularly in Latin America. The

1

semi-autonomous National Endowment for Democracy (NED) was established by Congress in that period and began to operate in many parts of the world. Democracy assistance grew rapidly in the late 1980s and early 1990s, as the Cold War ended and the global democratic trend spread dramatically to Central and Eastern Europe, the former Soviet Union, Africa, and parts of Asia. The Clinton administration has solidified the place of democracy promotion as one of the four core priorities of U.S. foreign assistance; during the past five years, several hundred million dollars of U.S. funds have been devoted annually to encouraging democracy's spread.[3]

The U.S. government is by no means the only actor in this growing field. U.S. private foundations are increasingly involved, especially in Central and Eastern Europe and in the former Soviet Union.[4] Democracy promotion is now on the bilateral assistance agendas (sometimes explicitly, sometimes as promoting "good governance") of many other Western countries, including Canada, Great Britain, Germany, Holland, Denmark, and Sweden. It is now also pursued by a number of multilateral organizations, including the United Nations, the European Union, the Organization for Security and Cooperation in Europe, the Organization of American States, and the Organization of African Unity.[5]

Since 1989, the former communist countries of Central and Eastern Europe have been an important focus of U.S. (and European) democracy assistance. The Bush administration responded to the fall of the Berlin Wall and the unanticipated collapse of communist systems around the region by committing the United States to helping support these countries' transitions to democracy and to market economics. The Clinton administration has continued that undertaking. U.S. assistance—economic, political, and humanitarian—has been a major element of this policy. In the first five years after 1989, the U.S. assistance effort, established under the Support for Eastern European Democracy (SEED) Act of 1989 as the Support for Eastern European Democracy Program, provided $1.69 billion of assistance for the former communist countries of Central and Eastern Europe. Although most of this assistance was economic and humanitarian, $110 million was devoted to democracy-related assistance programs.[6] In the same five years, the National Endowment for Democracy provided an additional $17.8 million of democracy-related assistance to the region. (Although the Endowment is almost exclusively government-funded, it is a semi-autonomous organization with an independent board of directors and

2

staff, and therefore its aid is not official U.S. assistance. For the purposes of this study, however, the Endowment's work is considered part of the general category of U.S. government-funded democracy assistance.)

In the initial period after 1989, U.S. democracy assistance to Central and Eastern Europe focused on what U.S. officials viewed as the most fundamental building blocks of democracy: constitutions and elections. U.S. assistance programs helped with drafting new constitutions and electoral laws, with the strengthening of administrative capacities of electoral commissions, and with sponsoring international election observation missions. As the wave of first-time elections passed, U.S. assistance was broadly diversified to include programs to help rebuild state and governmental institutions—particularly parliaments, judiciaries, and local governments—as well as programs to develop or strengthen non-state organizations and institutions such as trade unions, media, human rights groups, and civic education organizations. During the past two years, as the notion of civil society development has become increasingly popular among U.S. assistance providers, the non-state or "bottom-up" half of this overall effort has become the leading priority of U.S. democracy assistance in the region. In some countries, notably Poland and the Czech Republic, U.S. democracy assistance since 1989 has been built on the foundation of U.S. assistance to dissident groups and emerging socio-political movements of the 1980s. In countries that experienced no liberalization in the 1980s, for example Romania and Albania, the post-1989 democracy assistance represents a rapidly constructed world of new actors, relationships, and activities on both the donor and recipient sides.

Enough time has passed since 1989 to begin taking the measure of U.S. democracy assistance in Central and Eastern Europe. There is a strong need to assess the effects the assistance is having, how it is evolving in relation to events in the recipient societies, and how it is perceived and valued by people in the recipient countries. Such an assessment is necessary both to gain a full understanding of the transitions in the countries themselves and to improve the assistance for the future. Assessing U.S. democracy assistance in Central and Eastern Europe is also useful for understanding U.S. democracy assistance in other parts of the world, particularly in the former Soviet Union, where democracy assistance is in an earlier phase and is borrowing heavily on the methods and structures of assistance to Central and Eastern Europe. Because U.S. assistance, and Western assistance generally, is still relatively new to Central and Eastern Europe, many of the basic underlying assumptions and operational features of the assistance stand out in sharper relief there than elsewhere.[7] Central and Eastern Europeans are still asking hard questions about Western assistance— questions that too often have been assumed away in regions where assistance relationships with the West are measured in decades or even generations rather than months and years.

There is a notable lack of in-depth, field-oriented studies of U.S. democracy assistance to Central and Eastern Europe—or in fact of U.S. democracy assistance to any part of the world.[8] As a result, debates in Washington over the value and validity of such assistance tend to be sterile exchanges between inordinately hostile opponents who are convinced that such assistance is *a priori* a vain, misguided undertaking and enthusiastic proponents who are certain that such assistance is *a priori* of unquestionable utility. These debates have only superficial reference to the empirical realities of democracy assistance. They are uninteresting and uninformative to the large majority of the U.S. policy community and public, who tend to believe that such assistance is probably worth trying but who are nagged by doubts about whether it really accomplishes much.

Providers of U.S. democracy assistance do sometimes carry out evaluations of their own programs, generating some information about how such assistance is working in practice. Such evaluations are generally kept in-house by the assistance organizations, however, and thus do not contribute much to whatever wider pool of knowledge exists on the subject. In addition, these in-house evaluations typically have a number of features that limit their utility. They are usually performed immediately after a project is finished, and therefore shed light only on the near-term effects of the assistance. They also generally examine only one project at a time; they do not consider the overall set of U.S. democracy assistance projects in a country to compare the projects to each other or to assess the assistance as a whole. The evaluations usually focus on specific operational issues and only rarely identify or question the assumptions embedded in the assistance projects concerning the underlying model of democracy, the appropriate role of external actors in domestic political life, or other basic issues.

Furthermore, to the limited extent that the evaluations attempt to explore the perspective of persons within the recipient countries,

4

they generally focus only on beneficiaries of the assistance, who tend to tell official evaluators that the assistance has been well-directed and should be continued. The evaluations often fail to gain the views of others in the recipient society who have not participated directly in assistance projects but who are in a position to analyze and sometimes shape the sectors or issues in question. Similarly, the evaluations tend to look only at whether the intended effects of a program have been accomplished. They seldom search broadly to try to understand all effects of a program—intended or unintended, positive or negative, immediately appearing or later developing, and so on.

The category of persons who carry out official evaluations also constitutes a limiting feature. For USAID evaluations, at least, the evaluators frequently have little to no experience or expertise in the country in which the subject programs took place. Instead, they tend to be chosen more for their familiarity with the type of program or with USAID itself. It may be that for many economic assistance programs, such as agricultural or health projects, extensive knowledge of the country in question is not essential for evaluating effects. For politically related assistance programs, however, such knowledge is crucial. Moreover, the persons who conduct evaluations for USAID, though independent of USAID itself, are often part of a relatively close community of development professionals who work as contractors for USAID on a regular basis. As such, they are likely to share many of the basic assumptions of USAID staff about the methods and goals of foreign assistance and to produce evaluations that reflect rather than question these assumptions.

This study attempts to redress this general lack of knowledge about how U.S. democracy assistance, particularly to Central and Eastern Europe, works in practice. It examines U.S. government-sponsored democracy assistance programs in one country of the region, Romania, and attempts to offer a multi-dimensional analysis of the assistance. The study first presents an overview of the range of assistance programs in that country, an examination of the relation between democracy assistance and overall U.S. policy toward the country, and an assessment of each of the major types of democracy assistance carried out there. It then provides a general analysis of the effects of the assistance, the underlying strategies of democratization, the methods of implementation, and the conflicting perceptions of assistance providers and recipients, as well as a comparison of U.S. and European democracy assistance.

In the research for this study, I conducted approximately 150 interviews—the majority of them in Romania during the course of four trips there between October 1994 and October 1995. I spoke with a wide range of Romanians who have either participated in U.S. democracy programs or are knowledgeable about the sectors that the U.S. programs have touched. These persons included members of parliament, political party workers, judges, lawyers, trade unionists, journalists, civic activists, executive branch officials, professors, local government officials, university students, and businesspeople. I sought out a diverse mix of research contacts in terms of political affiliation, age, professional background, and degree of involvement with U.S. assistance organizations. Most of the research was conducted in Bucharest, because most U.S. democracy assistance has been implemented there, although I also conducted a significant number of interviews in two major provincial cities, Iaşi and Craiova. In both Washington and Bucharest, I also interviewed a number of Americans who have worked on democracy assistance programs in Romania representing most of the U.S. organizations that have been involved in such assistance. In addition, I interviewed a number of State Department and USAID officials who have served in Romania since 1989 and various U.S. and European academic specialists on Romania.

This research builds on previous experience I had in Romania, including a visit to the country in 1983 and numerous trips there in 1990-92 as an election observer and consultant for the National Democratic Institute for International Affairs. During the latter period, I gained many first-hand impressions of U.S. democracy assistance programs, impressions which I attempted to follow up on and deepen in my recent research trips. This study also builds on extensive work on U.S. democracy assistance that I have done in other parts of the world, particularly in Latin America, since 1985.

The study was specifically designed to avoid some of the limiting features of in-house evaluations. Aiming at a medium- to long-term perspective, the study looks at some projects years after they were completed. It attempts to assess the whole set of U.S. democracy assistance programs in the country under study, thereby permitting some comparisons of programs. The study specifically aims to identify and question the underlying assumptions in the assistance programs about democratization and the role of external actors. It is based on an extensive effort to ascertain the views of people in the recipient country. It not only examines the intended effects of assistance projects but also tries to determine the full range of effects of the various projects.

In assessing the effects of democracy programs, I very consciously utilized a qualitative rather than quantitative methodology, contrary to the trend among U.S. assistance providers of seeking quantifiable, reductionistic methods of program evaluation. With respect to the local institutions and sectors that have been the targets of U.S. democracy assistance in Romania, I attempted to develop a detailed understanding of how these institutions and sectors have or have not changed over the past five years. I pursued these inquiries using interviews with persons directly involved in or having some interest in such areas, reading relevant local studies and media reports, and personally observing the functioning of the institutions over time. As I gained an understanding of whether and how the various institutions and sectors were changing, I used similar methods of study and observation to try to determine the major causes of the changes (or lack of changes) and, in particular, the extent to which U.S. assistance programs have been a causal factor in those changes.

No one case of democracy assistance can reveal more than a very partial view of the overall world of such assistance. Nonetheless, in this complex realm, where answers to basic questions about the effects and value of such assistance lie woven into the fine-grained texture of the socio-political life of the recipient countries, single-country depth rather than multi-country breadth of analysis has important compensations. The case of Romania, moreover, is particularly interesting. U.S. democracy assistance projects in Romania are diverse and in their type and size generally typical of the democracy projects sponsored by the United States since 1989 throughout Central and Eastern Europe—and in fact in many countries of the former Soviet Union, Latin America, Africa, and Asia as well. Politically, Romania is a gray-area case—its democratic transition is neither moving forward nor backward very rapidly or clearly. Gray-area cases much better illuminate the strengths and weaknesses of democracy assistance than do societies that have moved rapidly to a successful democratic consolidation—or those which have lapsed from an initially positive transition back to some form of dictatorship. In gray-area cases, external democracy assistance is neither a dispensable supplement to a strongly self-propelled process nor a futile ricochet off an impenetrable wall. Instead, the assistance becomes more deeply drawn into the local processes of the attempted political transition, resulting in a more thorough testing of the strengths and weaknesses of the programs.

Furthermore, Romania has provoked particularly intense feelings among U.S. providers of assistance. For some Americans who have worked on democracy assistance projects in Romania, the experience has been deeply engaging and satisfying. Others have come away frustrated, disappointed, and angry. I have attempted in this study to avoid the discourse of extremes that marks both Romanian politics and the experiences of Americans who have worked in Romania. At the same time, I hope I have managed to convey a sense that democracy assistance is not an impersonal, technical discipline but an intensely human one involving myriad dilemmas, debates, and decisions as complex and absorbing as those of political life itself.

CHAPTER 2

POLITICS, POLICIES, AND ASSISTANCE

THE POLITICAL CONTEXT

THE LEGACY OF CEAUŞESCU

I t is impossible to understand the evolution of Romanian politics since 1989 without awareness of at least the most basic features of Nicolae Ceauşescu's rule.[9] After an initial period of relative moderation in the late 1960s and early 1970s, Ceauşescu imposed upon Romania an increasingly repressive, arbitrary, and dictatorial rule. Ceauşescu transformed the Communist Party apparatus into a tool of his erratic megalomania and reduced Romanian political life to a tragi-comic cult of personality centered upon himself and his almost equally powerful and capricious wife, Elena. Ceauşescu subordinated every organization and institution in Romanian society to his absolutist drive, and protected his power with an extraordinarily harsh, pervasive, and secretive internal security force—the notorious Securitate. Unlike all of the other communist countries of Central and Eastern Europe except Albania, Romania underwent no political liberalization during the 1980s. If anything, the terrible climate of fear and repression grew worse in those years. The few dissidents who emerged were relentlessly persecuted and either silenced or driven out of the country as Ceauşescu doggedly resisted the growing liberalization trend in the Soviet Union and other nearby communist countries.

Romania's backwardness was economic as well as political. Its economic deprivation during the 1980s was also worse than in any other Central or Eastern European country (again with the exception of Albania). The abysmal economic situation in Romania was the result of Ceauşescu's ruinous policies, which embodied the worst elements of communist economics carried to extremes— massive misallocation of resources to marginally useful heavy-industry projects, rigid central planning, a complete lack of rational production and distribution incentives, and so forth. Ceauşescu's idiosyncratic decision to pay back Romania's foreign debt in the

9

1980s despite Romania's terrible economic condition demanded even greater austerity from the already impoverished Romanian populace.

Ceauşescu's political cruelty and economic failures produced a highly demoralized, atomized society. Romanian citizens learned to distrust not only all forms of organized power but also each other. Shut off from the world, they were forced to waste their time in pointless jobs and to devote significant energy to circumventing continual scarcities and just getting by. By the end of the 1980s, Romania was deeply isolated, suffering under extreme political repression and horrendous economic deprivation, and subjugated by a dictator determined to carry forward his monstrous dynasty into the next century.

THE EVENTS OF DECEMBER 1989

At the 14th Communist Party Congress in November 1989, while the rest of the region was swept up in an exhilarating tide of anti-communist revolutions, Ceauşescu delivered a "no-compromise, no-change" address, reaffirming his complete rejection of even limited, gradual reforms. On December 15, in Timişoara in western Romania, a crowd gathered spontaneously to defend Laszlo Tokes, a minister who had spoken out on human and religious rights and faced eviction from his church. The crowd grew, and two days later, on Ceauşescu's orders, security forces attacked the demonstrators, killing many of them. Protests continued in Timişoara and began to spread around the country. On December 21, Ceauşescu spoke to an arranged rally of citizens in Bucharest. The rally unexpectedly turned into an anti-Ceauşescu demonstration, and battles broke out between the demonstrators and some of the security forces present. With demonstrations spreading in other parts of the city, Ceauşescu and his wife attempted the next day to address the crowd outside the Central Committee headquarters. Met with derision and a barrage of stones, they retreated into the building and fled from the roof by helicopter. That same day, a small group of prominent Romanians led by Ion Iliescu, a party official who had fallen out of favor with Ceauşescu in 1971, announced the formation of the Council for National Salvation (later the National Salvation Front) and declared themselves in charge of the country. The Ceauşescus were quickly apprehended and on Christmas Day were hastily tried by a makeshift military tribunal and executed.

Reflecting the exceptional features of Romanian communism, the Romanian revolution of December 1989 differed markedly from the anti-communist revolutions in other Central and Eastern European societies. It came about very suddenly, with no intermediate phase of liberalization or gradual political decompression. It was violent, with at least a thousand people killed in the fighting during December 1989. Most important, the revolution was not clearly a revolution at all. It did not entail the overthrow of the communist system in Romania but the ouster of a deeply despised dictator. The authorities who took power after his demise were in many cases persons closely linked to the previous system of power. Many Romanians believe that Ceauşescu's ouster was in fact a palace coup by a group of disaffected people within the party hierarchy who had been plotting against Ceauşescu for some time and who took advantage of the popular unrest in December 1989 to take power.[10]

EARLY 1990

Romanian political life since December 1989 has unfolded in three periods.[11] The first was the short, early transitional period from the overthrow of Ceauşescu to the elections of May 1990. In those hectic, often bewildering months, two main political developments occurred. First, the National Salvation Front, at the time a highly opaque, even mysterious organization, began to define its political character and ambitions. Some of the prominent anti-communist intellectuals who had joined the Front in the first flush of enthusiasm in December 1989 quit, hollowing out the image of the Front as a broad coalition of political forces and rendering it more clearly a group of former members of the communist system. The Front, increasingly confident of its position, reversed its original non-political line and announced its intention to compete in the upcoming elections.

The second main political development was that a number of organizations separate from and often opposed to the Front began to emerge. Some were political parties, both reestablished versions of the parties that dominated Romanian political life in the inter-war period (the National Peasant Party, the National Liberal Party, and the Social Democratic Party) and new entities (such as the Hungarian Democratic Union of Romania and the Romanian Ecological Party). There also emerged a wide array of small groups,

11

associations, and organizations, including new trade unions, student groups, associations of intellectuals, independent newspapers and magazines, human rights groups, and environmental organizations. Many of these groups consisted of only a handful of people and operated with almost no resources, but they nonetheless began to constitute a small, visible sector independent of the government.

Romania rushed into its first post-communist elections, held in May 1990, in a confused and still almost improvisatory state. The elections, to choose both a president and a legislature, were flawed in various ways. The Front systematically exploited its near-total hold on the reins of power to favor its own political campaign, manipulating the state television, utilizing state resources such as transportation and communication equipment, and relying on the still-active internal security forces to harass and sometimes inflict violence on opposition party candidates and activists. Most Romanians outside the major cities were only dimly aware of the existence of any political alternative to the Front. Despite the unfairness of the campaign and the procedural irregularities that occurred on voting day, the results were so decisive that most international observers accepted their basic validity. The leader of the Front, Ion Iliescu, was elected President with 85 percent of the vote. The Front received 66 percent of the vote for the Chamber of Deputies and 67 percent for the Senate.

FROM THE 1990 TO THE 1992 ELECTIONS

The second period of Romania's post-1989 political life, from the May 1990 elections to the local and national elections of 1992, began on an extremely low note. Several weeks after the May 1990 elections, President Iliescu ordered the police to break up the University Square demonstration, a two-month old peaceful occupation of one of Bucharest's main squares by students and other demonstrators protesting what they saw as the consolidation of a neo-communist system of power in Romania. In response to some incidents of violence between police and demonstrators and a call for help by President Iliescu, several thousand miners from the north came to Bucharest (or in the view of some analysts, were brought to Bucharest by the government), where they spent two days marauding through the city, savagely beating demonstrators and bystanders, and ransacking the offices of opposition parties and independent newspapers. The sickening spectacle of the miners' rampage greatly aggravated the already polarized state of politics

12

in Romania and tremendously damaged Iliescu's and the Front's already troubled international reputations.

In the two years following the debacle at University Square, Romania slowly, often haltingly, moved along a path of political and economic reform toward its next set of elections. President Iliescu eschewed any dramatic process of de-communization for Romania, emphasizing gradualism and an only partially coherent idea of emergent social democracy. The ruling powers undertook no searching inquiries into the communist past and left Ceaușescu's legacy a repudiated but still undigested weight on Romanian life. The government—led first by a young reform-oriented former communist, Petre Roman, and then (after Roman's ouster in September 1991 following another miners' incursion) by the technocratic Theodor Stolojan—did enact a number of economic reform measures. These efforts, which included an initial privatization program, a foreign investment law, a land reform program, and a new legal framework for the commercial sector, stopped far short of the sort of radical economic liberalization under way in other countries in the region, such as Poland. They nonetheless constituted the start of a process of transition to capitalism.

The political atmosphere in those years was still clouded by fear and uncertainty. The secret police were reined in somewhat and partially reduced, but not dismantled. Political intimidation and violence diminished, but infiltration and surveillance of opposition parties and other independent organizations continued. The major opposition parties nonetheless gradually expanded their organizations and activities, and formed a coalition (the Democratic Convention, later the Democratic Convention of Romania), raising the profile of the opposition around the country. In the media, the broadening of political debate was limited by the government's continued dominance of the state television channels and numerous obstacles to printing and distribution imposed by the government on independent newspapers. A wide range of opinions nevertheless could be and were expressed in the printed press and on the radio. In addition, the development of non-governmental organizations continued, slowly widening the socio-political space in Romania.

A new constitution was adopted by public referendum in late 1991. Local elections were held in February 1992, with the Front caught off-guard by opposition victories in a number of cities. In the spring of 1992, a long-simmering division over the pace of reform between former Prime Minister Petre Roman (who favored faster reform) and President Iliescu culminated in a splitting of the Front, with Roman forming his own party. Presidential and legislative elections were held in September 1992, with a presidential run-off election in early October. Iliescu was re-elected President for a four-year term, gaining 61.4 percent of the vote in the run-off against Emil Constantinescu, the candidate of the Democratic Convention of Romania. Iliescu's party led the parliamentary voting with approximately 28 percent of the vote, followed by the Democratic Convention (20 percent) and Roman's party (a little more than 10 percent). The other groups meeting the 3 percent threshold for representation in both houses of Parliament were three nationalist parties and the Hungarian Democratic Union. The campaign leading to the September 1992 elections was marked by continued illegitimate advantages for Iliescu's party, and the elections themselves suffered from procedural irregularities. Nonetheless they were a significant improvement over the May 1990 elections and were accepted by most international observers as generally free and fair.

SINCE 1992

The 1992 national elections were an important juncture in that they gained the Romanian government credibility in the West. They did not, however, mark any significant change in Romania's domestic evolution. Since 1992, Romania has continued on roughly the same hesitant road to reform. The long-term goals of democracy, capitalism, and membership in the European Union and NATO are repeatedly stated in public, but actual efforts to achieve those goals are often weak and uncertain. The opposition rejected Iliescu's offer in late 1992 to join his party (now called the Party of Social Democracy in Romania, or PDSR) in a coalition government, and the PDSR has since ruled in first an informal coalition and more recently and briefly in a formal one with the three small nationalist parties. (The formal coalition established in January 1995 partially broke up in October 1995.) The government, led by a colorless and poorly regarded Prime Minister, Nicolae Văcăroiu, can point to few accomplishments in the areas of sociopolitical or administrative reform. The Parliament has gained a general reputation for ineffectiveness and corruption. The economic situation has been improving since 1994, with inflation

14

greatly reduced and growth under way, thanks largely to a well-designed macroeconomic stabilization program imposed by the semi-autonomous central bank, the National Bank of Romania. Actual economic restructuring has moved slowly. The privatization of large-scale state enterprises is only now just beginning; banking reform has been very slow in coming; and the privatization of agricultural land, though largely accomplished, was poorly thought through. President Iliescu has remained somewhat detached from the daily issues of political life, concentrating his energies on an active and partially successful effort to burnish his and Romania's images in the West. Romania regained most-favored-nation trade status with the United States in 1993, was the first country in the region to sign up for NATO's Partnership for Peace program, and (also in 1993) gained admittance to the Council of Europe.

Political and economic power in Romania remains highly centralized, with the ruling party still exhibiting a dangerous tendency to blur the distinction between itself and the state. Power centers outside the ruling structures remain weak. The opposition parties have spent much of their energy on in-fighting and have not greatly strengthened their popular base or their political programs. The national trade union confederations also have been caught up in often bitter internecine rivalries and have not gained the strength their large memberships might imply. The media is diverse, with many new private television stations, radio stations, and newspapers, but the government maintains control over the sole national television station, which is by far the most influential source of news in the country. Non-governmental organizations (NGOs) operate actively in many socio-political fields, but they remain highly dependent on foreign funding and are still quite weak outside Bucharest and a few other cities.

Six years after the fall of Ceauşescu, Romania is a greatly changed society with many of the institutional features of democracy, a nascent capitalist economy, and an identifiable path toward gradual integration with Europe. At the same time, however, it lags badly behind many of its neighbors in clearly breaking away from the communist past. It has put off facing some of the most serious challenges of economic reform and seems unable to escape a turgid, polarized political life. Most Romanians feel the pain of rising prices and diminished security much more acutely than the benefits of incipient economic growth and are disgusted by the corruption and inefficiency of "democratic" politics; the bright future they hoped for in December 1989 still appears quite distant.

15

"HALF-EMPTY" OR "HALF-FULL"?

Most Americans interested in Romania (and in a more complex fashion Romanians themselves) tend to hold to one of two sharply conflicting interpretations of Romania's post-1989 evolution. Some take a negative view, seeing the partially filled glass of reform as half-empty. In this view, Romanian political life is divided between a neo-communist elite, essentially the old communist *nomenklatura*, holding firmly onto power, and a struggling collection of Romanian democrats who, through opposition politics or civic activity, seek to democratize the country. The adherents of this "half-empty" view acknowledge that some political and economic reforms have been made. But they argue such reforms have largely been enacted to please Western governments (and the International Monetary Fund), have almost all been partial, and often have been undermined by less visible contradictory measures. They believe that the real aim of Iliescu and the PDSR is to cement their hold on power by creating a Mexican-style quasi-democracy featuring a dominant ruling party with lucrative ties to state banks and state companies, a tolerated but very limited opposition, and electoral mechanisms but no actual alternation of power.

In this view, the only way democracy will come about in Romania will be the shattering of the *nomenklatura*'s hold on power through an opposition victory in national elections. Due to Romania's recent absolutist past and the weak state of civic education since 1989, most Romanians are highly vulnerable to manipulation by the ruling powers, rendering such a victory elusive. The opposition parties are continually thwarted by the government—harassed and infiltrated by the secret police, deprived of access to resources comparable to those of the PDSR, and forced to compete in manifestly unfair electoral campaigns.

The other view of post-1989 Romanian politics is a relatively positive picture, portraying the glass of reform as half-full rather than half-empty. The central tenet of this outlook is that what counts is overall direction, not the speed of reform, and that Romania's direction is right: President Iliescu and his party clearly have been moving Romania in the direction of democracy and capitalism since 1989. Iliescu has made mistakes, most notably permitting (or directing) the miners to come to Bucharest in June 1990, but on the whole he has been serious and successful in pursuing a path of gradual reform which has led to a relatively open, active political life in the country, a growing economy, and increasing international

16

recognition. The proponents of this "half-full" view contend that Iliescu should be given credit for guiding the country skillfully through a potentially unstable period of political decompression, for balancing the pressure for rapid change in some sectors of the population with the deep conservatism and outright fear of change on the part of many other Romanians. They also assert that those critical of the country's relatively slow pace of reform are failing to take into account the unusually harsh nature of communist rule in the past and are in effect blaming the current government for what is actually the legacy of Ceauşescu.

Proponents of the "half-full" view see the opposition in Romania as dominated by inept and often marginal figures who are generally unqualified to assume positions of power. They believe that the opposition parties are stuck in inter-war period mentalities and dominated by persons who, despite their democratic rhetoric, are just as often monarchists or petty autocrats as genuine democrats. They also attribute the opposition parties' electoral failures not to governmental machinations but to the organizational ineffectiveness of those parties, the weakness of their leaders, and the inability of the opposition to connect with Romania's large peasant and lower-middle classes.

Among Romanians, the "half-empty" and the "half-full" perceptions constitute the underlying psychological framework of the highly polarized national political life. It is extremely difficult for day-to-day politics in Romania to be useful or productive when the persons engaging in it share no common understanding about fundamental issues such as the basic direction of Romania's post-communist evolution and the legitimacy of the government. Within the U.S. policy bureaucracy, these two contending views of Romanian political life have co-existed uneasily since 1989. As analyzed later in this chapter, the contending allegiances to these views have been the main source of division and friction on Romania policy among U.S. policy-makers.

OVERVIEW OF U.S. DEMOCRACY ASSISTANCE TO ROMANIA

ORGANIZATIONS AND RELATIONSHIPS

Since 1989, U.S. government-funded democracy assistance to Central and Eastern Europe generally has been implemented through a three-level institutional framework. At the first level are the U.S. donor organizations, with the two main donors being the Agency for International Development and the National Endowment for Democracy. The U.S. Information Agency has also been active in this field, primarily on the education side, both with its own funds and as a recipient of USAID funds.

At the second level are the principal recipients of the funding from USAID and the NED, a collection of what can be called U.S. intermediary organizations. These are U.S.-based, non-profit groups that generally specialize in a particular area of democracy assistance, such as media, local government, or the rule of law. In Romania, they have included the Free Trade Union Institute (FTUI), the International Republican Institute (IRI), the National Democratic Institute for International Affairs (NDI), the International Foundation for Electoral Systems (IFES), the Central and East European Law Initiative of the American Bar Association (CEELI), the Institute for Democracy in Eastern Europe (IDEE), the National Forum Foundation, the International Media Fund, and the International City/County Management Association. As "core grantees" of the National Endowment for Democracy, FTUI, IRI, and NDI receive a significant portion of the NED's funds each year. They also receive USAID funding, which in recent years has been greater than their NED funding.

At the third level are the local organizations that work with the U.S. intermediaries. In Romania, such organizations have included the Parliament, trade unions, newspapers, radio stations, civic advocacy organizations, the Central Electoral Commission, mayors' offices, the Magistrates' School, and political parties. Most of the assistance provided to these local organizations has been in the form of training and technical assistance rather than grants. The U.S. intermediary organizations have delivered training, logistical assistance, strategic advice, visiting experts, informational materials, and small amounts of equipment to the organizations with which they work.

There are some exceptions to this general pattern. The Institute for Democracy in Eastern Europe makes small grants to local organizations, which in Romania have been primarily journals, newspapers, and civic education organizations. The NED devotes a small share of its overall funding to small, direct grants to local groups; in Romania these have primarily been non-governmental organizations (NGOs) concerned with civic education and human rights. USIA and USAID have in the past several years set up small grants programs for democracy assistance in Romania and other countries of the region. In the past two years USAID also has established the Democracy Network program, through which local NGOs can receive small grants as well as training and technical assistance.

THE TYPES OF ASSISTANCE

Prior to December 1989, there was almost no U.S. assistance, governmental or non-governmental, relating to the promotion of democracy or human rights in Romania. The complete absence of any liberalization movement in the country meant that Romania, unlike some other countries of the region, had no human rights groups, independent unions, environmental groups, or other entities that Western organizations could support. U.S. democracy assistance was limited to a few small grants to expatriate groups, such as NED's support for *Agora,* a quarterly intellectual journal in Romanian edited by prominent Romanian émigrés, and for the London-based Mihai Eminescu trust for independent cultural activities in Romania.

Since Ceauşescu's fall, U.S. democracy assistance to Romania has unfolded in three stages, corresponding to the three stages of post-1989 Romanian political life: from December 1989 to the May 1990 elections, from mid-1990 to the 1992 national elections, and from late 1992 to the present. The first stage was short and hurried. After the dramatic and quite unexpected events of December 1989 in Romania, the U.S. government scrambled to get some democracy assistance programs under way to support the political transition. USAID was not yet operating in Central and Eastern Europe, and so the SEED Act funds relating to democracy promotion went through the NED in 1990. In the early months of that year, representatives of various U.S. intermediary organizations—particularly NED core grantees such as the International Republican Institute, the National Democratic Institute, and the Free Trade Union Institute—traveled to Romania looking for potential partners and projects. Few of the Americans from these organizations had been to Romania before, and few of the Romanians they began to deal with had ever had any significant contact with Americans. The political atmosphere in Romania in this period was murky and still turbulent. Nonetheless, many of the American assistance organizations that went to Romania arrived at a common interpretation of the political situation and of the necessary focus of U.S. democracy assistance. They judged the events of December 1989 to be only a partial and potentially reversible political opening and

19

they were highly skeptical of the intentions of the ruling National Salvation Front. They concluded that U.S. assistance was crucial to help keep alive the possibility of a democratic transition and that such assistance should concentrate on supporting persons and organizations that seemed genuinely committed to challenging the Front.

Thus U.S. democracy assistance in this early period went to a number of new (or in the case of the opposition political parties, newly reconstituted) organizations, including the Group for Social Dialogue, a group of prominent Romanian intellectuals formed immediately after the Revolution and modeled loosely on the Czech Civic Forum; *Frăţia*, the first independent trade union to emerge after 1989; the Romanian Students League, a new student organization that quickly emerged as an outspoken voice against the government; the newly reestablished pre-communist era political parties, the National Peasant Party, the National Liberal Party, and the Social Democratic Party; *România Liberă*, the largest new opposition newspaper; and the League for the Defense of Human Rights (LADO), the first highly visible, post-1989 human rights organization. The immediate goal of much of this early assistance was simply to help these organizations become operational before the May 1990 elections, so that there would be opposition forces present in the electoral process and alternative political messages available to the population. In addition, NDI and IRI mounted an international election observer mission for the May 1990 elections.

After the Front's decisive victory in the May elections and the miners' rampage in Bucharest in June, many U.S. donors and intermediaries stopped to debate the value of continuing to work in Romania, but most decided to go ahead. The next round of elections became a focal point for a number of assistance programs. IRI carried out a major project to assist the main opposition coalition, the Democratic Convention, with party-building and campaign activities. NDI supported the creation and development of the Pro Democracy Association, a Romanian non-governmental organization devoted to democratic civic education whose main activity in the 1990-92 period was putting together (in conjunction with LADO) domestic election monitoring programs for the local and national elections of 1992. IRI and NDI jointly sponsored international election observation missions for the 1992 local and national elections. And the International Foundation for Electoral Systems provided technical assistance to the Romanian Central Electoral Commission.

In this period, a number of other democracy-related assistance projects were initiated or continued. The Free Trade Union Institute gave significant assistance in 1990 and 1991 to *Frăția*, the trade union confederation. The International Media Fund began working with the newspaper *România Liberă* to make operational the large printing press purchased with U.S. funds in early 1990—a task that took several years to complete. The International Media Fund also invested considerable resources in trying to help Romania's first private television station, SOTI, to get started. The human rights bureau of the State Department, together with USIA, sponsored a rule-of-law program that included technical assistance to the constitution-drafting process and various educational activities designed to foster the idea of judicial independence and the rule of law generally. The American Bar Association's CEELI program, also emphasizing the rule of law and judicial reform, got under way in Romania in 1992. USIA sponsored visitor programs to bring Romanians to the United States to gain exposure to institutions and political processes relevant to the operation of democracy. The Institute for Democracy in Eastern Europe and a few other U.S. organizations provided modest support to various Romanian non-governmental organizations involved in civic education and human rights, as well as to various small independent newspapers, radio stations, and magazines.

Since the 1992 national elections in Romania, U.S. democracy assistance has shifted away from its electoral emphasis. IRI has continued with some training for the opposition parties, but it has devoted more effort to a parliamentary strengthening program. NDI has continued to work with the Pro Democracy Association, but that group has broadened its focus to include a range of civic education activities. With the dismantling of the Central Electoral Commission (it was created only as a temporary body for the 1992 elections), IFES moved from election administration to supporting NGO development.

Other assistance programs launched in the 1990-92 period have generally continued since 1992, with some modifications or changes of emphasis. FTUI continues to try to promote independent trade unions, but it now offers training to a wider variety of unions and, for reasons discussed in the next chapter, has replaced *Frăția* as its main partner with a different confederation, the National Union Bloc. The International Media Fund moved from its projects with *România Liberă* and SOTI to a smaller training program for

21

journalists before ceasing operations in 1995. CEELI continues to carry out various legal-sector programs relating to judicial training, legal education, and the rule of law generally. IDEE continues giving grants to small newspapers, journals, and other media or cultural organizations. USIA has broadened its range of democracy-related programs to include book translations, scholarships, visitor exchanges, and other education-related efforts. One new democracy-related program since 1992 involves local government: USAID has funded the International City/County Management Association to carry out a project to help strengthen the technical capacity of mayors in several cities. A new effort is the Democracy Network program, run in Romania by World Learning, Inc., a U.S. NGO, to provide training, technical assistance, and small grants to policy-oriented Romanian NGOs.

As detailed in Table 1, USAID and the NED funded approximately $13.5 million of Romania-related democracy assistance projects between 1990 and 1994. USAID's Romania democracy funding was about ten times that of the NED's, a proportion approximately equal to that between USAID and NED democracy programs worldwide. These funding figures highlight the main priorities of U.S. democracy assistance in Romania: media, elections, political parties, unions, and civic advocacy NGOs. They also underline the dominance of a relatively small number of Washington-based NGOs, particularly core grantees of the NED (which in Romania operated much more with USAID funds than NED funds), among the recipients of the U.S. assistance.

PRIVATE U.S. DEMOCRACY ASSISTANCE

In most other countries of the region, especially Poland, the Czech Republic, and Hungary, U.S. government-funded democracy assistance has been complemented by parallel efforts underwritten by U.S. private foundations, such as the Ford Foundation, the Pew Charitable Trusts, and the Rockefeller Brothers Fund. However, with two main exceptions—the Soros Foundations and the German Marshall Fund of the United States—U.S. private philanthropies have stayed away from Romania, at least with respect to political development work (many private U.S. organizations have been involved in charitable work, particularly concerning orphanages, in Romania). The reasons for this avoidance are rarely made explicit. They seem to relate to the common U.S. perception of Romania as a laggard with respect to political and economic

Table 1. ROMANIA-RELATED FUNDING FOR DEMOCRACY PROJECTS, 1990-94[a]: USAID AND NED (thousands U.S. dollars)

Organization		1990	1991	1992	1993	1994	Total
USAID FUNDING							
International Media Fund		350	1,584	521	337	275	3,067
National Democratic Institute (NDI)		437	1,084	389	0	279	2,189
International Republican Institute (IRI)		200	428	384	204	408	1,624
USIA		0	391	177	199	560	1,327
International Foundation for Electoral Systems[b] (IFES)		142	511	260	0	299	1,212
CEELI		0	0	53	100	137	290
USIA (Rule of Law)		0	106	96	0	0	202
Other[c]		462	0	146	42	238	888
USAID AND NED FUNDING							
Free Trade Union	AID :	297	0	388	202	350	1,237
Institute	NED :	0	224	150	117	154	645
(FTUI)	Total :						1,882
Institute for	AID :	100	72	0	0	0	172
Democracy in	NED :	0	0	281	0	8	289
Eastern Europe (IDEE)	Total :						461
Foreign Policy	AID :	100	0	0	0	0	100
Research Institute	NED :	17	58	35	0	0	110
(FPRI)	Total :						210
NED FUNDING							
Romanian NGOs		0	40	25	0	135	200
				USAID Total			12,308
				NED Total			1,244
				USAID and NED Total			**13,552**

[a]Figures provided by USAID and the NED. Years are fiscal years. USAID figures are for actual obligations of funds. The NED figures are for grants approved. In 1990, the NED administered USAID's democracy-related assistance to the region.
[b]Of IFES's 1990 funds, $11,000 came from the NED rather than USAID.
[c]Includes funds to Northeastern University, Freedom House, German Marshall Fund, Graceland College, and other U.S. institutions, primarily for media, human rights, and minority-related programs.

reforms—and, more generally, to Romania's image as an especially difficult, opaque, and somehow disagreeable socio-political environment.

The absence of most major U.S. foundations from Romania is unfortunate. Romania needs their assistance—as much and probably more than most other countries of the region. U.S. government-funded democracy assistance programs would likely have benefited from operating alongside a greater number of privately funded projects, as they would have been able to see first-hand the more flexible (and often more locally sensitive) implementation methods of such institutions. A more equal mix of public and private U.S. democracy assistance also would help break the pervasive Romanian habit of assuming that all assistance coming from the United States is a direct expression of White House and State Department intentions and views.

The Soros Foundations have been by far the largest private philanthropic actor in Romania. The Soros Foundation for an Open Society-Romania was established in June 1990 (based in Bucharest with branch offices in Cluj, Timişoara, and Iaşi) and currently has an annual program budget of over $10,000,000. The main areas of Soros-Romania's programming have been education, civic society, science and medicine, and arts and culture. The Soros Foundations do not organize their programming around the concept of democracy promotion but rather around the idea of openness; in Romania, their goal is to help Romanian society be both more open to the West and more open internally.

Much of the civic society programming of Soros-Romania is similar, at least in general focus and purpose, to the civic society side of U.S. government-sponsored democracy assistance. A major thrust of Soros's civil society programming has been the development of independent media; in this domain, Soros-Romania is the largest donor organization operating in Romania. The other two main emphases of its civil society programming are human rights and ethnic conflict. Although similar in overall focus and purpose to U.S. government-sponsored civil society programs, Soros-Romania's civil society programs, and in fact all its programs, are structured and implemented in ways that differ significantly from U.S. assistance. In the section on implementation in Chapter 4, the many positive aspects of Soros's approach in Romania are discussed.

The German Marshall Fund of the United States has funded an extensive set of activities relating to political development in

Romania since 1990. The main emphasis of this programming has been promoting human rights and citizen participation. Most German Marshall Fund grants have gone directly to organizations in Romania, primarily to independent human rights organizations. The total of German Marshall Fund grants for Romania from 1990 to 1994 was $640,000 (including a $100,000 small-grants program funded by USAID and operated by the German Marshall Fund).

THE PLACE OF DEMOCRACY ASSISTANCE IN U.S. POLICY

ASSISTANCE AND POLICY

In principle, U.S.-funded democracy assistance programs are an integral part of U.S. policy. In practice, however, the relationship between democracy assistance and policy is not always consistent. Complexities and even contradictions may arise because of conflicts within the policy bureaucracy over the compatibility of democracy promotion with other U.S. interests. Or problems may result from disagreement among policy-makers about how the goal of democracy promotion should be pursued. Or the U.S. officials involved in providing assistance and those formulating broader policy may disagree over how closely U.S. assistance should conform to the overall diplomatic line of U.S. policy.

The case of Romania reflects some of these complexities. On one level, the place of democracy assistance in U.S. policy toward Romania since 1989 appears straightforward. The U.S. government has sought to support a democratic transition in Romania, and democracy assistance has been one way of doing so. A closer look, however, reveals that tensions among U.S. officials have sometimes arisen over democracy assistance, and that the situation has not always been one of a simple consonance of assistance and policy. The question of the relationship between democracy assistance and policy is explored in this section, as part of a general analysis of U.S. policy toward Romania since 1989.

POST-1989 U.S.-ROMANIAN RELATIONS: THE REGIONAL FRAMEWORK

The background to U.S.-Romanian relations in the post-1989 period is of course the special relationship that Romania enjoyed with the United States and other Western countries from the late 1960s into the 1980s as a result of Ceauşescu's foreign policy independence from the Soviet Union.[12] Obsessed with the idea of himself as an international statesman and of Romania as a significant player in international affairs, Ceauşescu devoted enormous amounts of energy to cultivating his favored position in Western diplomatic circles. U.S.-Romanian relations did, however, eventually deteriorate during the second half of the 1980s, as the growing U.S.-Soviet rapprochement reduced the importance of Romania's maverick foreign policy and the stagnant repressiveness of Ceauşescu's rule grew increasingly out-of-step with the liberalization trend in the Soviet Union and other communist countries.[13] The single most tangible sign of this deterioration was the termination in 1988 (by Ceauşescu's unilateral action in anticipation of a U.S. move to terminate) of the agreement establishing most-favored-nation trade status for Romania (a status originally granted in 1975 as a mark of Romania's favored position).

U.S. policy toward Romania since the overthrow of Ceauşescu is best understood as one case of a generally consistent U.S. policy toward the former communist countries of Central and Eastern Europe since the fall of the Berlin Wall. The Bush and Clinton administrations have pursued a policy of helping these countries carry out transitions to democracy and to capitalism, or, in the shorthand expression that has gained currency among U.S. officials, to helping these countries become "market democracies." The rationale for this policy is that successful transitions to democracy and capitalism in Central and Eastern Europe will be favorable to U.S. interests because "market democracies" make better economic and security partners of the United States and will expand the community of peaceful democratic nations.

This broad regional context of U.S. policy toward Romania since 1989 has been difficult for many Romanians to appreciate, conditioned as they are by the Ceauşescu years to believe that U.S.-Romanian relations are of special importance to the United States compared to U.S. relations with other countries in the region. The fact that the United States has paid more attention to (and given more assistance to) some other countries in the region, such as Poland, has been hard for many Romanians to accept.

The post-1989 policy of the United States toward the former communist countries of Central and Eastern Europe has been implemented with a traditional "carrot and stick" approach. The United States has offered diplomatic attention and praise, technical and financial assistance, and trade benefits to those countries moving ahead with political and economic reforms, and withheld or reduced such benefits to those countries perceived as stagnating or backsliding. Given that most countries of the region moved fairly decisively and early toward reform, U.S. policy has been largely carrot rather than stick. As the clear laggard during the first few years after 1989, Romania was the country toward which the United States tried hardest to exert pressure to move more clearly toward democracy and capitalism.

ESTABLISHING THE POLICY

In the first few months of 1990, U.S. policy toward post-Ceauşescu Romania took shape quickly. The Bush administration reacted in a positive though cautious way to the overthrow of Ceauşescu. The administration was pleased to see Romania join the regional trend toward democracy but was concerned about the violence that accompanied Ceauşescu's fall and about the obviously incomplete, uncertain nature of the transition. Secretary of State James Baker stopped briefly in Bucharest on his way from Prague to Sofia in February 1990 and conveyed to Romania's new leaders the U.S. interest in their carrying forward a real transition to democracy and capitalism. He focused on the issue of elections, which the Bush administration saw as the key test of the National Salvation Front's democratic intentions. He also met with a group of opposition politicians, putting on his hat as a campaign strategist and talking with them about political campaign strategy. In the ensuing months, Secretary Baker and other U.S. officials pressed the Romanian leadership to schedule early elections, to ensure that those elections were free and fair, to permit independent media to operate, to allow international observers at the elections, and to not interfere with newly established U.S. assistance programs involving the fledgling opposition groups. These programs were a crucial element of U.S. policy toward Romania in this initial period.

Although the Bush administration quickly and clearly settled on a policy of promoting a transition to "market democracy" in Romania, divisions within the administration began to emerge almost immediately over how to interpret the political situation in post-Ceauşescu Romania. A majority of the White House and State Department officials concerned with Central and Eastern European affairs subscribed to an early version of what has been characterized above as the "half-empty" view of Romanian political life. They saw the Front as dominated by ill-willed neo-communists and

27

viewed the emergent opposition as the key hope for democracy in Romania. A much smaller number of U.S. officials in Washington (the most prominent of whom was Richard Schifter, then Assistant Secretary of State for Human Rights and Humanitarian Affairs), along with a majority of the higher-ranking officials at the U.S. embassy in Bucharest, held to an early version of the "half-full" view. They believed that the Front was genuinely committed to a process of meaningful political and economic reform, and they were skeptical of the capacities and significance of the emergent opposition forces. They also saw the ascendancy of the Front as a useful means of undercutting the strength of newly emerging nationalist groups.

These two outlooks pointed to different policy prescriptions. Those who held the "half-empty" view tended to believe that the best way for the United States to support a democratic transition in Romania was a policy of strong pressure on the government to undertake democratic reforms coupled with vigorous support for the emerging opposition sector. Those who held to the "half-full" view felt that to promote democracy, the United States should be generally supportive of the Romanian government, acting as a helpful partner rather than a critic, and should not invest much hope or attention in the opposition. In early 1990, the "half-empty" view strongly dominated U.S. policy. As discussed below, it continued to do so for several years, although the other view made itself felt at various junctures.

TAKING SIDES

After the flawed May 1990 elections and the horrifying miners' rampage in June of that year, U.S.-Romanian relations sank to a low point. The Romanian government did win credit with the Bush administration through its strong support in the U.N. Security Council for the U.S. position during the Iraq-Kuwait crisis in August 1990 (Romania held the presidency of the Security Council at that time). But the basic framework of U.S. policy established in early 1990 was unchanged: the United States sought to exert pressure on the Romanian government to undertake democratic reforms and to support the emerging sector of persons and organizations independent of (and usually opposed to) the ruling power structures.

After an internal policy review in mid-1990, the administration settled on four benchmark objectives that the Romanian government would have to meet before U.S.-Romanian relations could be normalized: 1) holding free and fair elections; 2) permitting the development of independent media; 3) respecting minority rights; and 4) reducing the activities of the Securitate. The restoration of most-favored-nation (MFN) trade status for Romania, an issue of moderate economic importance but of tremendous psychological importance to Romanians, came to be defined in both Bucharest and Washington as the key element of a normalization of U.S.-Romanian relations—the reward that would come when Washington was satisfied with Romania's political path. From 1990 through 1992, the issue of whether and when to restore Romania's MFN status produced endless debate and struggle within the Bush administration as well as between Congress and the administration.

Of the four benchmarks, free and fair elections were the most important to the Bush administration and received the most attention in the 1990-92 period. The administration decided that it could not simply hold out the MFN "carrot" and hope for free and fair elections. Instead, it would actively help "level the playing field" in the next Romanian elections—that is, it would try to make up for some of the material and structural disadvantages the Romanian opposition faced vis-à-vis the Front. U.S. support for the opposition took various forms. Some was moral and diplomatic—for example, meetings between Romanian opposition leaders and U.S. officials in Washington and Bucharest in which U.S. officials communicated their sympathy for the opposition's cause. Some support was strategic and technical. USAID funded a program in which the IRI provided equipment, training, and counseling to the Democratic Convention from 1990 through the 1992 local and national elections. Although this assistance to the opposition was carried out by an intermediary organization, U.S. officials viewed it as an intrinsic part of U.S. policy. As one State Department official involved in Central and Eastern European affairs commented in an interview, "the Republican Institute operated at the edge of the envelope. They carried significant water for us in Romania and elsewhere in the region." Furthermore, many other U.S. democracy assistance programs in those years, such as aid to the opposition paper România Liberă and the new private television station, SOTI, were clearly intended to benefit the opposition even though they did not consist specifically of assistance to the opposition political parties.

The public line of U.S. policy was that the United States merely supported free and fair elections and sought only to help assure a legitimate process, not to influence the outcome. The actual policy, however, which U.S. officials acknowledged only privately, was to help increase the chance of a victory by the Romanian opposition. Most U.S. officials—and most of the Americans working for the various U.S. organizations involved in democracy assistance programs—had no qualms about the United States taking sides in the Romanian electoral process. They saw the elections as a contest between democratic and non-democratic forces and believed that what they considered the non-democratic forces held many advantages deriving from their position of power. In this view, therefore, it was necessary for the United States to play a partisan role in the elections in order to further the goal of promoting democracy.

Yet not all U.S. officials agreed with this approach. Those who subscribed to the "half-full" view of Romanian politics accepted the goal of free and fair elections but argued that Romania should not be held to unrealistically high standards that took no account of the country's unusually difficult past. They felt strongly, moreover, that the U.S. government should avoid taking sides. They disliked many of the U.S. democracy assistance programs, particularly the IRI effort, because of the pro-opposition nature of the programs. During these years, officials skirmished frequently over the policy, with the proponents of the "half-full" view fighting an uphill battle to soften the policy of pressure against the Romanian government and to reduce the partisan nature of the U.S. involvement in the electoral process. Given the close ties between democracy assistance programs and the main thrust of U.S. policy, this skirmishing inevitably at times extended to the assistance programs.

In early 1992, for example, tensions arose within the U.S. government over how to monitor the upcoming local elections in Romania. Those elections were to be the crucial test for U.S. policy purposes of whether the Romanian government met the free and fair election standard (after a fight among U.S. policy-makers over whether the local or the national elections were supposed to be the test). The International Republican Institute and the National Democratic Institute decided to field a joint observer delegation (with USAID funding), as they had in May 1990. The U.S. embassy in Bucharest, dominated by officials holding a relatively sympathetic view of the Romanian government, saw IRI as reflexively hostile to the Romanian government and not to be trusted to produce a balanced assessment of the elections. The embassy countered by organizing its own observer delegation and, after the elections, arguing that its delegation's more positive assessment of the elections should be given greater weight than the assessment of the IRI-NDI delegation.

A TURNING POINT

The 1992 local elections proved to be a turning point in U.S. policy toward Romania. The Bush administration accepted the elections as having been generally free and fair and began to move toward a normalization of U.S.-Romanian relations. U.S. officials who had backed the policy of pressure on the Romanian government generally believed there were still serious democratic deficits in Romania. Most of these officials also felt, however, that the lever of withholding MFN status could not be applied usefully much longer and that the Romanian government had met the benchmarks set out by the U.S. government for better relations. In the months after the local elections, the Bush administration initiated the process of restoring MFN status (a process that moved slowly during the rest of the year, primarily due to conflicting views within Congress).

The period between the 1992 local and national elections in Romania saw a transition in U.S. policy, but a transition that was not always consistent. On the one hand, the Bush administration was moving away from the earlier policy of pressure toward a policy of normalization. With the local elections having already put Romania over the free and fair elections threshold, the national elections were of reduced importance in general U.S. policy terms. On the other hand, many U.S. officials in Washington were still sympathetic to the opposition and believed the United States should actively support it in the hope of an opposition victory over Iliescu. Meanwhile, the U.S. assistance programs set in motion in 1990 and 1991 concerning the elections were in full gear. The IRI in particular was heavily involved in the opposition coalition's campaign, sending a special full-time political strategist to Bucharest in mid-1992 to help the Convention. It would be too much to say that the democracy assistance programs, with their intensive focus on the national elections and their generally pro-opposition character (with some exceptions, such as the IFES election administration project and NDI's support for the Pro Democracy Association), were out of sync with U.S. policy in the period leading up to the 1992 national elections. More accurately, they represented a policy line that had enjoyed dominance earlier, and they continued to operate somewhat on their own momentum even as they were eclipsed by the broader evolution of U.S. policy.

31

NORMALIZATION

The 1992 national elections gave an additional strong push to the process of normalization of U.S.-Romanian relations. The weak showing of Emil Constantinescu, the Democratic Convention's presidential candidate, and the relatively free and fair nature of the electoral process consolidated the view within the U.S. government that it was time to stop treating Romania as the black sheep of the region. Since late 1992, U.S.-Romanian relations have been on a mostly steady upward path. An early landmark on that path was the restoration of MFN status for Romania in early 1993. Another was Romania's being the first country to sign up for NATO's Partnership for Peace program in January 1994 and the resultant growing U.S.-Romanian military cooperation. President Iliescu came to Washington in 1993 for the opening of the U.S. Holocaust Memorial Museum and visited President Clinton briefly in the Oval Office. Iliescu returned to Washington in September 1995 for a working visit and had a round of meetings with President Clinton, Vice President Gore, and a number of top administration aides. The U.S. government does still occasionally express its displeasure about particular domestic acts by the Romanian government, such as the firing of many opposition party mayors in 1994 and early 1995. But in general the U.S.-Romanian relationship is positive, and U.S. government officials do not involve themselves much in Romania's domestic politics.

Two divergent views of Romanian politics still do exist within the U.S. government, although the division is now rather muted. At the U.S. embassy in Bucharest, the relatively positive, "half-full" view of the Romanian government predominates. In this view, the U.S. policy of normalization is clearly the correct course. Among policy-makers in Washington, the "half-empty" view of Romanian politics is the dominant although not the only view. Proponents of the "half-empty" view tend to see the policy of normalization as not especially pleasing but nonetheless inevitable—given a lack of means by which the United States can exert pressure for faster reform in Romania and the fact that other countries in the region are no longer uniformly ahead of Romania on the reform path.

U.S. democracy assistance in Romania has partially conformed to the overall policy shift from pressure to normalization; since 1992, it has become somewhat less oriented toward the partisan, pro-opposition approach. The shift is only partial, however. IRI, for example, still carries out a political training program open only to opposition parties. A number of the U.S. intermediary organizations working on democracy assistance in Romania still operate from a stark black-and-white view of the political situation and interpret their task narrowly as strengthening the political opposition and groups generally sympathetic to the opposition. This discrepancy between the continuing partisan nature of some U.S. democracy assistance programs and the normalization thrust of overall U.S. policy inevitably causes puzzlement and frustration among Romanian officials. Faced with what they perceive as mixed signals from the U.S. government, they tend to assume that assistance programs are an unimportant, misplaced footnote to the high-level diplomatic track of presidential visits, security cooperation, and the like. Similarly, the assistance-policy gap produces an attitude of indifference and even scorn toward the assistance programs among at least some U.S. embassy officials, who are generally strong adherents of the "half-full" view of Romanian politics. They end up seeing democracy assistance not as part of U.S. policy but as the independent work of USAID or of U.S. intermediary organizations with private agendas in Romania.

ASSISTANCE AND POLICY: ORGANIZATIONAL RELATIONSHIPS

Two different organizational relationships underlie the way U.S. democracy assistance in any particular country relates to the overall U.S. diplomatic policy line toward that country. One is the relationship between the State Department and USAID. For most forms of U.S. foreign assistance, the State-USAID relationship is a fairly limited, formalized pattern of arm's-length cooperation. Democracy assistance poses special challenges in this regard. Such assistance concerns the politics of the recipient country, an area in which the State Department rather than USAID has dominant expertise. Yet at the same time, State Department officers usually have little experience with the issue of how external assistance can be brought to bear on a political transition process, a subject about which at least some USAID officers are beginning to accumulate knowledge. The need thus exists for close collaboration between USAID and State on democracy assistance, both at the embassy level and in Washington. In some countries, such collaboration has developed. In others, such as Romania, it has not—due either to the personalities of the relevant officers or to substantive differences of opinion over the local political situation and/or the forms

33

democracy assistance should take. In such cases, democracy assistance efforts derive little benefit from the State Department's political expertise and may be adversely affected by inter-bureaucratic tensions or a lack of support from the State side.

The other organizational relationship, or set of relationships, directly bearing on the assistance-policy issue are those between the U.S. government agencies funding democracy assistance, primarily USAID, and the U.S. intermediary organizations that implement the assistance. As with the issue of State-USAID relations, democracy assistance raises special challenges in this domain. On the one hand, USAID must maintain a close enough relationship with the intermediary organizations to ensure the basic conformity of their activities with U.S. policy. On the other hand, the intermediaries need enough freedom to operate without constant micromanagement and with genuine flexibility. When the assistance is highly political (as much democracy assistance is) and when the intermediaries are organizations with their own very individual, visible political profiles (such as IRI, NDI, and FTUI), these two imperatives are not easy to balance. And as sometimes has been true in Romania, when the democracy assistance is openly partisan and some of the intermediary organizations have views of the local political scene that differ from the dominant view within the U.S. government, the assistance-policy relationship can become problematic. U.S. officials underestimate these problems when they fail to consider either the political viewpoints held by U.S. intermediary organizations or the tendency of persons in the recipient countries to assume that because U.S. intermediaries are operating with U.S. funds, their activities are a direct expression of U.S. policy.

CHAPTER 3

FOCAL POINTS OF THE ASSISTANCE

This chapter examines seven major areas of U.S. government-funded democracy assistance in Romania—assistance concerning political parties, elections, rule of law, parliament, civil society, trade unions, and the media. Taken together, U.S. assistance in these categories constitutes most, although not all, of the overall U.S. democracy assistance effort in Romania since 1989. The analysis of each area begins with a short overview of the U.S. interest in the particular type of assistance, the situation in Romania regarding that sector, and a description of the relevant U.S. assistance programs. The analysis then concentrates on the effects of the assistance.

POLITICAL PARTIES

ASSISTING POLITICAL PARTIES

Prior to the 1980s, U.S. assistance to foreign political parties was largely a covert, Cold War tactic. In the 1950s and 1960s, the CIA secretly funneled money to foreign political parties, such as the Liberal Democratic Party of Japan, whose political success the CIA judged to be favorable to U.S. geopolitical interests.[14] One motivation behind the establishment of the National Endowment for Democracy in the early 1980s was to create an overt funding source for U.S. assistance to foreign political parties, and one that would be less closely tied to U.S. foreign policy. Since the mid-1980s, two of the core grantees of the National Endowment, the International Republican Institute and the National Democratic Institute, have been engaged in assisting political parties in many parts of the world. Initially, they carried out their work almost exclusively with NED funding. Gradually, however, USAID has overcome its reticence about political party assistance (a reticence that was principally based on the political sensitivity of the practice), and has increasingly been funding the party programs of IRI and NDI.

The political party work of both IRI and NDI tends to be relatively similar in content: it seeks to help foreign political parties 1) strengthen their internal organizational structures, 2) better understand the role of political parties in a democratic society, and 3) campaign more effectively using the techniques of political parties in established Western democracies. The basic assumptions of such work are that strong political parties are essential to a democratic political system, and that in transitional countries, external support for political parties (particularly training) can help transform weak parties into strong ones.

Although IRI's and NDI's political party work is generally similar in content, it often differs in approach. In most though not all cases, NDI's party work is multi-partisan and is offered to all political parties in a particular country. IRI, in contrast, often has taken a more partisan approach. In some cases, for example in many Latin American countries in the second half of the 1980s, IRI has worked with only one party in each country—the party whose ideology IRI believes most closely resembles the ideology of the Republican Party. In other cases, as in some countries in Eastern Europe and the former Soviet Union, IRI assists a particular group of parties, the parties IRI sees as clearly committed to democracy, in societies where some of the major parties or political forces are of uncertain democratic intent.[15]

POLITICAL PARTIES IN ROMANIA

In the initial period after the fall of Ceauşescu, the situation of political parties in Romania was highly fluid and uncertain. As mentioned earlier, in a dominant position was the National Salvation Front, an opaque, even mysterious political entity that had almost seamlessly gained the reins of power in December 1989 and that represented only a very uncertain and obviously partial break with the past. In addition to the Front, many new political parties were forming. Several of these were reconstituted versions of the three main political parties of pre-1939 Romania—the National Peasant Party, the National Liberal Party, and the Social Democratic Party, led by Romanians who returned to political life after 1989 from prison or abroad. Dozens of other parties were formed in this period (73 participated in the May 1990 elections), though most were very small operations, often consisting of just a leader and a few followers. Only a few of these new entities, such as the Hungarian Democratic Union and the Civic Alliance Party, were significant and lasting enterprises; most have faded away over the years.

From 1990 through 1992, there were several major developments in the evolution of parties. As discussed in Chapter 2, the National Salvation Front proved unable to overcome its internal divisions over the appropriate pace of reform. In early 1992, it split into what is now the main governing party, the Party of Social Democracy in Romania and the Democratic Party (recently merged with the Social Democratic Party). The number of opposition parties decreased substantially, to approximately ten significant parties. A coalition of opposition parties formed, bringing together most of the major opposition parties for the 1992 local and national elections as the Democratic Convention (later the Democratic Convention of Romania).

Since 1992, few major changes have taken place among the Romanian parties. The political spectrum appears to have settled somewhat with one large party, roughly of the center-left (the PDSR); a set of opposition parties whose ideologies range fairly widely from Social Democratic to Christian Democratic; and three small nationalist parties (viewed by many as extremist and antidemocratic). The Democratic Convention no longer comprises most of the opposition parties; following a series of defections during the past year, it now consists only of the Peasant Party and a few small closely allied parties.

THE U.S. ASSISTANCE

In U.S. assistance to political parties in Romania, IRI has been the major actor. NDI decided early on to focus on civic education, judging the lack of it in Romania to be a more fundamental problem than the weakness of the political parties. IRI has followed an openly partisan approach, assisting only the opposition in the belief that these parties represent "the democratic forces" of Romania and that the PDSR and the three nationalist parties are anti-democratic. The larger framework of IRI's partisan approach in Romania is the ardent anti-communism that IRI has brought to its involvement in Central and Eastern Europe and the former Soviet Union. IRI interpreted the political situation in Romania after December 1989 in black-and-white terms and has held to that interpretation ever since. As one IRI representative involved in IRI's early work in Romania in the aftermath of December 1989 said to me when asked to define IRI's mission there, "We saw Romania as one last chance to stick it to the Soviet Union."

37

In early 1990, IRI established contact with Romanian opposition parties, primarily the Peasant Party and the National Liberal Party. It rushed to carry out training and deliver equipment to help those parties prepare for the May 1990 elections, but its main push centered on the next major political battle, the 1992 local and national elections. IRI assumed the role of adviser, supporter, and most active foreign friend of the Romanian opposition parties. From mid-1990 through September 1992, it organized an extensive series of training seminars for the opposition parties, covering a wide range of topics relating to party-building and campaigning, including media usage, message development, fundraising, recruiting, and organizational methods. IRI also donated office space and equipment for eleven communications centers for the Democratic Convention around the country. IRI staff members and consultants who worked in Romania in those years describe their relationship with the opposition parties in vivid terms as a hand-holding protectorate in which savvy U.S. political operators showed inexperienced Romanians the political ropes. "We taught them what to say, how to say it, and even what to wear when saying it," one IRI representative told me. "They were like children. They were at the sixth grade level politically."

IRI worked not only to strengthen the opposition parties but also to foster opposition unity. IRI representatives "jawboned" the opposition leaders on the need for unity and organized many meetings to bring them together. When the National Liberal Party decided to split from the Democratic Convention in 1992, IRI representatives in Bucharest responded immediately, though unsuccessfully. "We basically locked all the party leaders in a room and tried to get them to work out an arrangement," an IRI representative told me.

IRI's work peaked in 1992 in the period leading up to the national elections. The special adviser sent by IRI in mid-1992 to help the Convention threw himself into the task of energizing a set of disorganized, often passive parties. He mounted an intensive series of training seminars, wrote campaign strategy memos to the Convention leadership (one memo, leaked to the press, caused a minor scandal), and traveled around the country exhorting opposition party activists to make a maximum effort in the campaign.

IRI's goal in 1992 was to help the opposition defeat President Iliescu. In private, IRI representatives made no secret of their desire to beat the governing power, a goal they saw as precisely equivalent

to promoting democracy in Romania. In public, however, IRI representatives described their role in Romania with the same phrase
commonly used by U.S. officials talking about U.S. policy generally:
IRI aimed to "level the playing field" in Romania's elections, to
counterbalance the advantages held by the National Salvation Front
stemming from its ties to the old communist power structure and
its ability and willingness to use state resources in its own behalf.
The concept of leveling the playing field was appealing to IRI and
to the U.S. government because it implied that IRI's role, though
openly partisan, was not to try to influence the results of Romania's
elections but to help give all parties an equal chance.

Since the 1992 elections, IRI has continued to assist the Convention, though in a much less concentrated fashion. From 1993
to late 1995, it sponsored approximately ten training seminars for
opposition party activists on party-building methods. As was the
case from 1990 to 1992, these seminars were generally led by
visiting U.S. political consultants. As discussed below, since 1992,
IRI has also developed a multi-partisan parliamentary assistance
program which it carries out in parallel to its party assistance work.

THE FRUSTRATIONS OF PARTY ASSISTANCE

Most of the IRI representatives who worked in Romania between
1990 and 1992 came away highly frustrated. Once the 1992
national elections were over, IRI staff and consultants spoke in
disparaging terms about the opposition parties, criticizing them as
inept organizations led by prima donnas unwilling to learn from
outsiders. Having set for itself the quite tangible goal of helping
the Democratic Convention win the 1992 national elections, IRI
felt after those elections that it had a clear failure on its hands. IRI
representatives, at least in private, blamed the opposition parties
for that failure.

Instead of using electoral results (which were undoubtedly
the product of many complex causal factors) to assess IRI's work,
it may be more useful to look at the overall evolution of Romanian
opposition parties from 1990 to 1995. In 1990, the fledgling opposition parties had a number of serious problems: 1) they devoted
significant time and energy to infighting; 2) they had no leaders
with wide public appeal; 3) they had little reach outside Bucharest
and a few other cities; 4) they were internally autocratic organizations dominated by older leaders who stifled the role of younger

activists; and 5) they did not have clear, well-conceived party programs.

Now, almost six years down the road, these problems are still very much present. The leaders of the opposition parties still engage in seemingly endless infighting and still lack broad popularity. A few opposition parties, most notably the Peasant Party, have broadened their reach outside the major cities, but in general the opposition parties are still urban, elite-oriented organizations with little real strategy for attracting Romanians outside the cities and the educated classes. Some of the parties have become more internally democratic and are beginning to permit a greater role for younger activists, but autocratic internal structures and pre-World War II mindsets are still common. Finally, the opposition has failed to counter government proposals with well-conceived alternatives on many of the key substantive issues—with occasional exceptions, such as the recent debate over the law establishing the second mass privatization program.

It is possible that the opposition parties will do better in the 1996 elections than they did in 1992—but only if President Iliescu stumbles badly in some way, or if the economic situation worsens drastically. That is to say, the next elections could be lost by Iliescu and his party through some (at this point) unexpected failing, but they are unlikely to be won by the opposition parties on the basis of their own political skills and strengths.

In sum, neither the IRI assistance nor that of the many Western European political parties operating in Romania has significantly strengthened the Romanian opposition. The assistance has exposed many opposition politicians and party activists to Western political ideas and methods and it has undoubtedly helped the parties begin to improve their party-building and campaign methods. But it has not altered the numerous fundamental weakness of the parties.

Why has the IRI assistance not had more marked positive effects? A number of overlapping explanations bear consideration. First, politically related training programs sponsored by external actors rarely achieve dramatic results. Americans involved in foreign assistance, particularly democracy assistance, often invest training programs with unrealistic expectations. Based on the assumption that democracy is the "normal" political form, Americans slip into the belief that simply exposing people in another country to U.S. political methods through a series of seminars will change lifelong patterns of behavior and thought. A related argument is that there simply has not been enough time yet to effect major changes in the Romanian opposition parties through external assistance. When asked about the apparently low level of results of their party work in Romania, IRI representatives argue that the parties are gradually becoming stronger but that, given the lack of any liberalization process in Romania in the 1980s, the Romanian parties are far behind their counterparts in other countries of the region and will require decades to develop into modern political parties.

A second explanation, one articulated by a number of Romanians who have participated in IRI training events, is that the training has not always been well designed. These participants are critical of the basic foreign-expert seminar method that has been the backbone of IRI's assistance. They find that many of the visiting experts know little about Romania, seem to view their visits to Romania as exotic travel adventures, and present information that is perhaps valuable in the United States but not well tailored to the Romanian context. Romanian participants single out for praise the few trainers who came back to Romania several times—not just because those trainers got to know the country better, but because they transmitted a feeling of genuine concern for Romania in their work. Romanian participants also criticize the seminar method as involving concentrated doses of information but few follow-up activities to help Romanians incorporate the information into actual practice.

If one looks at the Romanian parties themselves, a third, perhaps more fundamental cause of the weak effects of the assistance can be identified. IRI's assistance has been based on the idea that the Romanian opposition parties are basically weak versions of Western-style political parties that just need to be strengthened. Arguably, however, the Romanian opposition parties were not in 1990 and still are not much like political parties in the Western sense of the term. They are more what might be called political clubs—small, personalistic organizations in which a group of followers surrounds one or several leaders. The main function of such clubs is to provide a position of power and prestige to the leaders and a sense of group identity to the members. They are not seriously committed to becoming broad-based organizations with internally democratic structures seeking to define or occupy a significant space on the ideological spectrum.

Training members of such organizations in the techniques and methods of conventional Western political parties tends to

41

have little effect because the training is ill-matched to the basic nature of the recipient organizations. The necessary task is not really that of *strengthening* the Romanian opposition parties but of fundamentally *altering their nature*—something IRI's approach was not really designed to do. The point is not that there were obvious, readily available forms of assistance that IRI could have carried out to remake the Romanian opposition parties, but just that a basic gap has existed in the U.S. political party assistance between the nature of the training and the nature of the parties themselves.

UNINTENDED EFFECTS

IRI's assistance to the Democratic Convention has been a visible, often controversial form of U.S. involvement in Romania's political life, particularly prior to the 1992 national elections. In discussing this assistance with Romanians, I became aware that whatever intended effects the assistance has had with respect to strengthening the opposition parties, it also has had a number of unintended effects of equal or greater significance.

To start with, IRI's efforts have contributed to a siege mentality among some Romanian officials. The only type of foreign support for Romanian political parties that most people within the Romanian power structure had any familiarity with prior to 1989 was the Soviet model of assistance—that is, assistance as a means of political manipulation and control. It was natural, therefore, for some Romanians, upon hearing of U.S. aid for the Democratic Convention, to assume that such assistance involved secret deals, secret money, and the subordination of the Convention to U.S. dictates. The belief that they were being ganged up on in the elections by the richest country in the world, as well as by a host of other Western countries providing assistance to the opposition parties, helped Romanian officials justify to themselves the structural advantages they enjoyed in the electoral campaign deriving from their control of the state apparatus. Such advantages, in their own minds, were just *their* means of "leveling the playing field" in response to the actions of powerful external forces favoring the other side.

Within the top circles of the Romanian government there has been a more detailed understanding than at other levels of the power structure that the U.S. assistance to the Democratic Convention has been relatively modest in scope. The assistance has nonetheless provoked negative emotions at this high level as well.

I asked a number of persons close to the top circles of power how they felt about U.S. government aid to their political opponents in the 1992 elections and about the continuation of such aid since 1992. Their answers highlighted three points. First, they do not like the assistance and believe it to be interference in Romania's internal affairs. Second, they put up with it because they see it as just one small, bothersome part of their overall relationship with the United States—a relationship of great importance to Romania. And third, they did not and do not feel especially threatened by the opposition and have always doubted that external assistance to the opposition would make much difference. In the words of one former senior Romanian official, "Your assistance to the Convention made me wonder, how could a big, sophisticated country like the United States back such losers?"

A second unintended consequence of the assistance, at least during the 1992 national elections, was some strategic miscalculation by the opposition. IRI viewed Romanian politics as a clearcut struggle between anti-Western neo-communists and pro-Western democrats. IRI representatives encouraged the opposition (many of whom shared this black-and-white view) to highlight this duality in the electoral campaign. The moralistic, anti-communist line proved to be ineffective for the opposition in 1992 and has only locked significant parts of the opposition into a ritualistic, divisive approach to politics since—an approach IRI has continued to foster with its insistence that Romanian politics is still clearly divided into "democratic forces" and a non-democratic government. The opposition's emphasis in 1992 on their closeness to the West (for instance, the Convention used the U.S. Statue of Liberty as the dominant symbol in its main campaign poster) largely backfired. It helped Iliescu successfully play upon underlying nationalist sentiments, insinuating that the Convention was serving foreign interests and that he was the true protector of Romania's national interests.

A third unintended effect of the political party assistance by IRI and Western European parties is that it has contributed to the development of a "passive dependency syndrome" among at least some in the opposition. Despite the fact that IRI's assistance to the Convention has been greater than U.S. political party assistance in most other Eastern European countries, many opposition-party activists feel terribly neglected by the United States relative to what they think political parties in other countries of the region have received. Moreover, even though most U.S. officials involved in

Romanian affairs in the early 1990s believe that the United States went very far, even too far, in supporting the Romanian opposition, many within the opposition are bitter about what they perceive as a poorly fulfilled U.S. commitment to them. The IRI assistance to the Convention was intended to energize the opposition parties, to stir them up and get them out working full-time to build their political base and develop their organizational structures. Yet in part because of the heavy-handed, "take charge" approach of a number of IRI's consultants and representatives working in Romania in the early 1990s, the IRI assistance conveyed to some in the opposition parties the idea that the United States would make sure they got into power; the result is lassitude and an almost paralyzing bitterness over the imagined failure of the United States to do what they expected it to do.

A fourth unintended consequence of the IRI program concerns effects on other U.S. assistance programs in Romania. One distinctly partisan U.S. assistance effort almost inevitably colors other politically related U.S. assistance programs. Apart from those few Romanians who have been deeply involved in U.S. democracy assistance projects and know well the many different U.S. organizations involved, most Romanians tend to see all U.S. organizations operating in Romania as part of an undifferentiated set—"the Americans"— and assume that they are all interrelated agents of a unified U.S. policy. Thus the fact that "the Americans" are explicitly favoring the opposition parties in one program allows or encourages Romanians to think that other U.S. democracy assistance programs are part of the same partisan policy. This issue is particularly important in the area of civil society assistance, where a number of U.S. organizations have been striving to promote the idea of nonpartisan civic activity but many members of the Romanian power structure are skeptical of the idea, seeing it as a cover for oppositional politics.

ELECTIONS

ASSISTING ELECTIONS

Elections assistance has been the most common form of U.S. democracy assistance in the past ten years. The U.S. government responded to the wave of transitional elections in Latin America in the 1980s with frequent electoral observation missions and technical assistance to electoral authorities. As first-time elections spread to Asia, Africa, Eastern Europe, and the former Soviet Union, U.S. elections assistance became a regular pattern. Its popularity as a method of U.S. democracy promotion is not hard to explain. Americans often hold to a highly procedural conception of democracy in which elections figure as the single most important mechanism; elections, moreover, are easily suited to assistance programming. They are discrete, highly concentrated events that involve a relatively limited set of technical issues and that may have significant impact in a short time. In addition, election observation missions (a major element of many elections assistance efforts) are an "easy sell" in Washington, given that they usually involve at least some well-placed Washingtonians traveling to interesting countries for brief, engaging periods.

The U.S. government sponsors technical assistance to foreign electoral authorities for the purpose of improving the basic administration of the elections. Election observation missions are expected to serve two purposes. First, they are a means of gathering information about foreign elections—about the electoral law framework, the conditions of the campaign, the voting process, and the acceptance of the results by the participating parties—with the information usually made available to the U.S. government, the media, and the interested public. Such information is often crucial to determinations by the U.S. government and others as to whether particular elections were free and fair. Second, these missions are intended to reduce electoral fraud, the assumption being that a government holding elections will be less likely to commit fraud if it knows that election observers will be present. Election observation missions, therefore, are intended to be useful both to the United States and to the countries to which they are directed.

U.S. ELECTIONS ASSISTANCE IN ROMANIA

The U.S. government has provided assistance for the three major elections in Romania since 1989. For the May 1990 elections, two U.S.-funded observer groups were present: a 70-person multinational delegation jointly sponsored by IRI and NDI, and a small, official delegation led by Governor Garrey Carruthers of New Mexico. For the 1992 local elections, as discussed in Chapter 2, there was a large joint IRI-NDI observer delegation and a smaller observer team sponsored by the U.S. embassy. For the 1992 national elections, the International Foundation for Electoral Systems provided some technical assistance to the Romanian electoral authorities, and a joint IRI-NDI delegation observed the elections. In addition, the Romanian Pro Democracy Association (with funds and technical support from NDI) and LADO, a Romanian human rights organization (with funds from several U.S. organizations and technical support from the International Human Rights Law Group) jointly mounted a large-scale domestic monitoring effort during both the 1992 local and national elections. Through these efforts, approximately 5,700 Romanians observed the local elections, and 5,400 observed the national elections.

EFFECTS

The technical assistance provided by IFES to the Central Electoral Commission was useful concerning selected issues relating to the administration of the elections, particularly the training of poll workers. The impact of IFES's efforts was limited by factors beyond IFES's control—the fact that the Electoral Commission was formed relatively late and thus did not have much time to incorporate the assistance, and that the Central Electoral Commission was not especially interested in the assistance. The significance of these efforts was also diminished in a broader sense by the fact that the technical competence of the Romanian electoral authorities was not the main problem to start with; the principal issue with regard to the administration of the elections was the good faith of the political authorities—something not directly affected by technical assistance.

The presence of numerous U.S. and European observers caused the Romanian government to try to improve the organization and administration of the various elections, particularly the 1992 local and national elections. President Iliescu and Prime Minister Stolojan knew that a positive Western assessment of those elections was crucial to the Romanian government's quest for legitimacy in the West. They therefore tried to ensure that the election administration was technically competent enough so that the foreign election observers would leave with a positive impression. Some Romanian critics of the government argue that this effort was little more than a superficial show for foreigners. They assert, for example, that while foreign observers in 1992 were granted good access to pose questions to members of the Central Election Commission, Romanian journalists, civic activists, and opposition party representatives were not. Similarly, they say that copies of the 1992 Romanian electoral law were for some time easier to obtain in

English than in Romanian, reflecting the government's eagerness to please the foreigners and its indifference to aiding Romanians. Critics also highlight that the Romanian government's receptivity toward electoral observers was narrowly limited to foreign observers; the government was ill-disposed toward domestic election observers.

It is very difficult to determine the extent to which the U.S. election observation missions and those from other Western countries actually deterred fraud in the different elections. The answer to that question lies with persons who might have been planning to commit fraud, and they are obviously unlikely to volunteer such information. It is important to bear in mind that although one of the main purposes of election observation missions is to deter fraud, the actual ability of most election observation missions to do so is relatively limited. Foreign observer delegations usually cover only a small percentage of the polling stations in a country and generally for only a short amount of time at each station. Other than the small number of electoral assistance efforts that entail helping local groups organize a parallel vote count, coverage of the vote counting tends to be particularly weak. In many cases, most members of the observer delegations leave the subject country before vote counting and tallying is even finished (as was the case with U.S. observer missions in all three Romanian elections). Such missions may be able to uncover gross, systematic fraud, but not much more.

The various U.S. observer missions to the Romanian elections in 1990 and 1992 did succeed in gathering a great deal of information about the elections, and this information was certainly used by the U.S. government, media, and policy community in their efforts to understand and evaluate the elections. The Romanian experience highlighted some general limitations or shortcomings of the findings of international election observer missions. One problem is that different observer groups sometimes reach different conclusions about the same events—as occurred in 1992, when the joint IRI-NDI delegation and the delegation organized by the U.S. embassy came up with fairly different assessments of the local election process.

Another problem is that an observer delegation's finding of an absence of gross fraud in an election—often the most precise finding possible, given the limitations observer missions face in detecting fraud—can easily be misinterpreted. Because the results in the Romanian presidential elections in 1990 and 1992 were so lopsided, the IRI-NDI delegations felt that, having found no evidence of gross fraud, they could conclude that the basic direction of the official election results was valid. In the 1992 parliamentary elections, however, the results were less clear-cut (Iliescu's party gained just 8 percent more of the vote than the Convention, and several parties fell just above or just below the 3 percent threshold for parliamentary representation). The U.S. observation mission's finding of the absence of gross fraud thus said less about the validity of these results. But this distinction was generally lost on the U.S. media, on some U.S. officials, and on many Romanians, who interpreted statements by U.S. and other foreign observation missions of an absence of any finding of *gross* fraud as a certification that the elections were free of *any* fraud.[16]

A further problem with at least some international election observation missions is a tendency to focus on the events of voting day much more than on the other parts of the overall electoral process, such as the campaign period and the legal framework of the process. In many transitional elections, particularly those in which a fledgling opposition is challenging a strongly entrenched party with close ties to a formerly non-democratic state, the problem is not so much the threat of massive fraud on voting day as serious inequities in the campaign favoring the governing party. As noted previously, this was the case in Romania in 1990 and 1992. The most significant factors bearing on whether the elections were free and fair resided not in the events of election day but in the campaign period—the dominance of television by the governing party, the use of state resources in the campaign of the governing party, the harassment and intimidation of opposition party candidates and activists, and other similar issues.

The joint IRI-NDI observation efforts, more than most of the other foreign observation missions, did give attention to the overall electoral processes, not just the voting days. Yet a lack of clear standards in this area rendered it difficult to integrate this information into the narrow, voting day–oriented framework that governments, the media, and the policy community use to determine whether a particular election is free and fair. For example, would the fact that the opposition parties have some but not completely equal access to the media, and that the governing party is using some state resources for its campaign and subjecting opposition party activists to a moderate though not heavy degree of harassment render an election not free and fair? No definite answer to this question exists. In the absence of clear standards, the international community tends to apply a very lenient norm: as long as there is not massive, obvious fraud or severe administrative chaos on election day, an election will usually be accepted as legitimate by the international community even if the ruling party benefited from some systemic advantages in the campaign period.

ROMANIAN PERCEPTIONS OF U.S. ELECTION OBSERVATION

In 1990, U.S. election observers were warmly welcomed by the Romanian opposition parties and only grudgingly admitted by the Romanian government. In the spring of 1995, the head of the Democratic Convention, Emil Constantinescu, expressed doubts about the utility of international observers for the 1996 elections. Around the same time, Adrian Năstase, head of the Chamber of Deputies and a leading figure in the PDSR, stated in Washington that U.S. and other foreign observers would naturally be welcome at the 1996 elections. What caused this striking reversal of views from 1990 to 1995?

The disillusionment of the Romanian opposition with U.S. election observation missions started early. In 1990, many Romanians, especially in the opposition, attached enormous, almost obsessive importance to the judgment of the West about Romania's first post-communist elections. As mentioned above, two main U.S. missions observed the May 1990 elections—a small official delegation and a larger joint IRI-NDI delegation. The official delegation, in addition to being very small (six persons), spent less than three days in the country; its leader, Governor Carruthers of New Mexico, had no experience relating to observing elections or to Romania. Despite the very serious problems with both the campaign and the administration of the elections, on the morning after the elections, Governor Carruthers announced at a press conference that "in our view it was a proper election. The actual process yesterday was an accurate one and a good one."[17] Although that same day the IRI-NDI delegation issued a much more critical assessment, and four days later the State Department concluded that "serious distortions" marked the elections, the Carruthers statement was all that most Romanians heard.[16] The Romanian government, ecstatic over the Carruthers statement, had it repeated over and over on the national television and reproduced in banner headlines in the pro-government newspapers. The Romanian opposition parties were

49

astonished and enraged by the statement, and many persons within the opposition became permanently disillusioned with international election observation on the basis of that one crucial incident.

The disillusionment only grew in 1992. Many within the opposition parties were simply convinced, generally without much tangible evidence, that the 1992 presidential and parliamentary elections were stolen by the government. They disagreed fervently with the relatively positive assessment of those elections made by the IRI-NDI delegation and other observer groups. By this time, the opposition had seen enough of the workings of most international observer missions to fuel their already negative view of them. In particular, they were bothered by the fact that most observers arrived only a few days before an election and left the day after, that observers stayed in the most expensive hotels, and that most observers knew little about Romania and seemed to regard their observation missions as travel adventures.

The Romanian government has followed a virtually opposite evolutionary path in its attitudes about foreign election observation missions. Many in the Romanian power structure began in 1990 with a strong skepticism about foreign election observers, seeing them as troublesome meddlers in Romanian political life and an insult to Romania's self-respect. But experience with the official U.S. delegation in 1990 and with almost all of the foreign observer groups in the 1992 elections demonstrated the great utility of such missions to the government in its quest for international acceptance. Although at some level the idea of having foreign observers for the 1996 elections probably rankles many Romanians in the power structure, they are now relatively confident that such observers will be more useful than bothersome.

One element of the U.S. election observation efforts that Romanian officials single out for criticism is IRI's dual, simultaneous role in the 1990 and 1992 elections as both a supporter of the opposition and an observer of the elections. Romanian officials reasonably question whether an organization actively assisting one set of parties in an election should be accepted as a neutral observer of that election. They emphasize that IRI was asking the Romanian government to trust IRI to be neutral despite its partisan role with the opposition at the same time that IRI itself was questioning the Romanian government's neutrality with respect to the administration of the elections—a stance that Romanian officials found insulting.

DOMESTIC MONITORS

In talking with Romanians about election observation missions in Romania since 1989, I was struck that the two domestic election-monitoring efforts carried out in the 1992 local and national elections made a greater impression on many politically active Romanians than did any of the various international monitoring missions (with the singular exception of Governor Carruthers's May 1990 delegation). One of the factors contributing to this impression appears to be the much larger size of the domestic monitoring missions (thousands rather than dozens of observers)—and the resultant expectation that such missions have much more capacity than international missions to deter fraud. Another factor is that such missions are planned and carried out by Romanians rather than foreigners. Domestic monitoring has much less of the surface-skimming quality that marks international observer missions. Accordingly, it stirs up much stronger feelings, both positive and negative.

The attitudes of politically active Romanians about domestic monitoring are the reverse, in partisan terms, of their attitudes about international election monitoring. The Romanian opposition parties, though highly skeptical at first of the idea of the domestic monitoring efforts (with some prominent opposition party activists believing that domestic monitoring should be the work of the political parties, not civic groups), learned to value them. Many opposition activists credit the domestic monitors with having been crucial to the opposition's relative success in the 1992 local elections. The leaders of the opposition parties now strongly favor having domestic monitors at the 1996 elections. Among members of the power structure, on the other hand, the domestic monitors were widely resented and disliked in 1992 and were permitted primarily because of U.S. pressure on their behalf. Many Romanian officials saw the domestic monitors as troublesome agents of the opposition parties masquerading as neutral observers. The government has made unfavorable comments about the possible role of domestic observers in the 1996 elections, although it will probably seek to avoid a negative international response by permitting them in some limited form rather than banning them altogether.

RULE OF LAW

AN EMPHASIS ON LAW

Many Americans view the rule of law as a fundamental element of democracy. In the American view, laws not only hold a

51

society together; when properly enforced by an independent judicial system, they are the crucial bulwark that checks the power of the executive and legislative branches of government. Moreover, Americans view courts as a potential mechanism of significant socio-political change; such was the case in the United States with respect to the civil rights movement in the 1950s and 1960s.

Given this perspective, when Americans examine the state of democracy in countries undergoing political transition, they usually find many shortcomings in the rule of law: laws are not consistently obeyed, the judicial system is not truly independent, many laws are outmoded, and legal education is formalistic. The result is that programs aimed at judicial and legal reform often are part of the package when democracy assistance efforts are formulated.

The first major U.S. legal assistance effort abroad was the Law and Development Program funded by The Ford Foundation and USAID in the 1960s and 1970s. This was a large, multifaceted program whose primary goal was attempting to promote U.S.-style legal education and the use of law as a positive instrument of socio-political change in developing countries.[19] During the 1980s, USAID initiated a major judicial and legal reform program in Latin America, the Administration of Justice Program; from the mid-1980s on, it has been the dominant component of U.S. democracy assistance to that region. In the same period, the Asia Foundation has undertaken judicial and legal reform projects in many Asian countries. In response to the political events in Central and Eastern Europe in 1989, the American Bar Association established the Central and East European Law Initiative. With USAID funding, CEELI has carried out judicial and legal reform activities throughout the region.

THE RULE OF LAW IN ROMANIA

The Romanian legal system was completely Sovietized during the late 1940s and the 1950s. For forty years, it functioned as an integral element of a highly developed system of state repression. Although heavily bureaucratic, the state apparatus was lawless in many basic ways, rendering the law a politicized club wielded against citizens by their rulers. The judicial system was distorted by an overwhelming emphasis on the prosecutorial function, politicized and corrupted at many levels, and reduced to the same low degree of efficiency and responsiveness as all other parts of the communist state.

Since 1989, the rule of law in Romania has improved significantly. Serious shortcomings do remain, however, including: illegal behavior, particularly corruption by government officials; a common attitude at the higher levels of the power structure that the government and the state are above the law; and only weak institutional reform processes concerning both the law-making and law-enforcing processes. The judicial system has undergone partial reforms, including the creation of a Superior Council of Magistrates, the restoration of the pre-communist-era appeals courts, and the establishment of judicial tenure for at least some judges. Yet major problems remain. Prosecutors are still an overly powerful force, subject to political manipulation. High-level government officials still sometimes interfere with judicial proceedings. Judges' salaries are low, their work-related benefits have decreased, and their working conditions are poor. Corruption remains a concern, and the inefficiency of the judicial process is still daunting.

U.S. LEGAL ASSISTANCE

The U.S. government has sponsored two assistance programs relating to the rule of law in Romania. One program, carried out jointly by the State Department and USIA primarily between 1990 and 1992 (although USIA has continued some of the activities to the present), has consisted of varied educational activities and technical assistance relating to the rule of law—particularly judicial reform and constitution-drafting, visitor programs to the United States for Romanian judges and lawyers, visits by U.S. judicial experts to Romania, conferences in Romania focusing on legal issues, and law book donations.

The other program, run by the American Bar Association's Central and East European Law Initiative, is the focus of the analysis in this section. Since 1992, CEELI has been operating in Romania primarily through a series of U.S. local representatives (one or two at a time usually staying in the country for about one year) with support from CEELI's main office in Washington. CEELI's budget for Romania has been small compared to the budgets of some other U.S. intermediaries working on democracy assistance: between $100,000 and $150,000 in each of the past several years. Until mid-1995, the main emphasis of CEELI's work was an effort to promote judicial reform in Romania, in particular to foster greater judicial independence.[20]

To this end, CEELI has assisted the Romanian Magistrates' School, established by the Ministry of Justice in 1991 to provide training to newly hired judges and prosecutors. CEELI has donated materials for curriculum development to the Magistrates' School, sponsored seminars by visiting U.S. and other Western legal experts, and provided much informal support and advice. CEELI has also worked with the Romanian Magistrates' Association to help enable that organization to play a role in advancing judicial reform. It has also provided technical support for specific legal reform projects (furnishing analyses by U.S. law professors of draft Romanian laws) and for court administration reform.

In 1995, in response to the lack of significant progress on judicial reform and increasing local interest in other areas relating to the rule of law, CEELI began shifting gears. It has started to reduce its emphasis on judicial reform and to focus instead on providing assistance relating to commercial law reform and clinical legal education, and on aiding the Young Lawyers Association— a group of young lawyers interested in the modernization of private legal practice in Romania.

EFFECTS

CEELI's assistance to the Magistrates' School has been of minor help to a troubled and largely unsuccessful organization. CEELI's aid has strengthened the curriculum and been a source of moral support to those persons associated with the school during its many rocky periods. But the Magistrates' School faces serious problems that CEELI is not in a position to do much about. Fundamentally, the school is supported only superficially by the Ministry of Justice. Established at the initiative of a reformist Minister of Justice in 1991, the school has been left to dangle by the government after that minister left the government (that same year) and the push within the government for judicial reform largely died. In its fifth year of operation, the school still has no formal legal status, almost no permanent staff, minimal office and meeting space, and a weak reputation among judges and lawyers. The small doses of technical assistance that CEELI has been able to offer the school are of little significance next to these problems. The Magistrates' Association has been similarly problematic and CEELI's very modest efforts to aid the group have essentially bounced off an organization that was either unable or uninterested in making use of external technical assistance.

The overall effect of CEELI's work on judicial reform in Romania has been minimal. Even if CEELI's efforts with the Magistrates' School, the Magistrates' Association, and with court administration reform had borne fruit, they would almost certainly have had no more than a marginal effect on the overall state of the Romanian judicial system. The problems of the judiciary have roots in profound structural and contextual flaws—among them low judicial salaries; inadequate courtrooms, equipment, and materials; a lack of tenure for many judges; high-level political interference in judicial matters; and weak political will regarding judicial reform—upon which some improved judicial training and new technical knowledge about court administration are bound to have little effect.

Yet some parts of CEELI's programs and of the State Department/USIA rule-of-law project have had very modest positive effects. The assistance relating to the constitutional drafting process was valued by the Romanian participants. Technical assistance on specific legal topics, particularly in the commercial area, has conveyed information that has influenced the drafting of laws—although the final laws do not always reflect the influence of the technical assistance that went into the original drafts of the laws (as in the case of the disappointing bankruptcy law passed in mid-1995). Visits by Romanian judges and lawyers to the United States have helped expose them to new ideas about legal systems and in some cases have stimulated those involved to pursue small but worthwhile reforms in their immediate areas of operation.

RELEARNING THE LESSONS OF JUDICIAL ASSISTANCE

During the past ten years, the U.S. government, primarily USAID, has struggled with what has proved to be the very difficult task of assisting judicial and legal reform in Latin America. Although these efforts have had a record of only mixed success, some important lessons have been learned.[21] A review of CEELI's efforts in Romania reveals familiar obstacles being encountered in a different region and—after some expenditure of time, energy, and money—the same lessons being learned anew.

The main lesson that has emerged from U.S. judicial assistance efforts in Latin America is simple but fundamental: it is futile to provide judicial reform assistance to a ministry of justice or court system if the responsible authorities are not genuinely committed

55

to reform. This finding was recently highlighted in a major USAID-sponsored evaluation of judicial assistance worldwide.[22] External assistance cannot create a will to reform on the part of the relevant authorities; nor can it substitute for a lack of will to reform. CEELI began working on judicial reform in Romania when it still seemed that the initial impetus for such reform, evident in 1990 and 1991, might last. That impetus soon died out, however, leaving CEELI in the position of trying to help a system that was not especially interested in helping itself.

A second, related lesson is that problems of judicial independence and integrity tend to be more related to basic structural and contextual features (such as low judicial salaries and systematic political interference) than to a lack of understanding by judges of appropriate judicial values. The operational consequence of this lesson is that trying to foster judicial independence and integrity by organizing seminars for judges is bound to have little effect unless the assistance, and the local judicial and political authorities, tackle the more basic issues. CEELI's initial rationale for working with the Magistrates' School was that better training for judges would strengthen judicial independence. The weakness of this rationale, and of trying to change only one minor piece of the problematic situation of the judiciary, became obvious over time.

A third lesson is that judicial reform assistance is inevitably related to politics; it is not merely a technical undertaking. The idea of judicial reform as a technical, non-political process is appealing to Americans; it relates to the American vision of law as a special domain of self-standing principles and procedures set apart from the messy world of politics. Yet in a country where the judicial system has long been a tool of the political power structure, helping to wrest it out of the grip of the power structure is a profoundly political task. In explaining CEELI's effort to foster increased judicial independence in Romania, a CEELI representative emphasized to me that "we don't get involved in politics." Such hope for a non-political interpretation of judicial reform in Romania has proved illusory.

These three lessons have been progressively learned by CEELI in Romania. One can regret that they were not incorporated from the start, but it is a common phenomenon in the field of democracy assistance that lessons learned from experience in one region or by one organization have to be painstakingly relearned in other regions and by other organizations. CEELI's new focus on commercial law assistance, legal education, and the Young Lawyers Association represents a positive change. It is a response to what persons in the recipient country clearly want rather than what the United States thinks they should want. In its far more modest scope, it is also much more proportionate to the actual assistance resources available.

PARLIAMENT

THE U.S. INCLINATION TOWARD PARLIAMENTARY ASSISTANCE

For decades USAID has sponsored programs to foster the institutional development of national legislatures in other countries. Such assistance has multiplied in the past ten years as part of the general growth of U.S. democracy assistance. Parliaments seem to be almost irresistible targets for U.S. officials devising democracy assistance programs. They are highly visible, central institutions that often bring together the major political forces of a country. Parliamentary assistance promises large effects with relatively narrowly focused effort. Improving the main law-making body in a transitional society could in principle have far-reaching effects on the society as a whole. In addition, parliamentary assistance programs are usually easy to sell in Washington, particularly to the U.S. Congress, whose approval is often critical for funding. U.S. congressmen tend to respond positively to arguments that legislatures are fundamentally important to democracy and that institutional development of legislative bodies is needed in other countries.

The predilection for parliamentary assistance is rooted in the U.S. political model, in which the legislative branch is very strong and often quite independent of the executive branch. Using this model as their norm, American assistance officials analyzing the situation of democracy in other countries tend to conclude that the parliaments of most other countries are institutionally underdeveloped and overly subordinate to the executive branch. The fact that national legislatures in parliamentary systems are by definition much less independent than the U.S. Congress does not stop Americans from habitually concluding that foreign parliaments are too weak and need strengthening.

THE ROMANIAN PARLIAMENT

The first post-communist Parliament in Romania, elected in May 1990, had little legitimacy in the eyes of the international community because it was the product of flawed elections and was so heavily dominated by the governing party. Many Romanians also had a rather low opinion of that Parliament, although with Prime Ministers Petre Roman and Theodor Stolojan leading the government, it passed a number of significant economic reform laws. The Parliament formed after the 1992 elections had greater international and domestic credibility, at least initially, because of the improved quality of those elections and the wider representation of parties in the Parliament. The post-1992 Parliament has not, however, performed well. President Iliescu's party has exercised weak leadership in the Parliament. Relatively few laws of significance have been passed. The opposition parties have engaged in a reflexively negative rather than constructive oppositional mode. The Parliament has developed a reputation for monumental inefficiency and pervasive corruption; its deliberations have been broadcasted often on television, presenting Romanians with the discouraging spectacle of long, pointless debates, crude infighting, and parliamentarians of dubious character. Recent opinion polls indicate that Romanians hold their Parliament in lower regard than they do any other major societal institution, with 69 percent judging the activities of the Parliament to be "poor" or "very poor."[23]

PARLIAMENTARY TRAINING

In the period 1990 to 1992, U.S. democracy assistance in Romania was not targeted at the Parliament. The U.S. government focused on elections-related assistance, regarding the Parliament of that period as not worthy of institutional support. Romania was also left out of the large-scale U.S. assistance program—the Frost Committee Program—for Central and Eastern European parliaments launched by the U.S. Congress in those years.[24] After the 1992 elections, however, several different assistance programs relating to the new Parliament were initiated.

One multipartisan parliamentary assistance program, conducted by IRI since late 1993, aims generally to increase understanding among Romanian MPs about how legislatures function in a democracy. It also has the more specific aim of strengthening the committee system of the Parliament. IRI chose this latter objective in the belief that the Parliament spends too much time in unproductive plenary sessions and that it would be more effective if its committees had more authority and autonomy.

IRI also has been sponsoring a series of short training seminars for Romanian MPs at which visiting foreign experts present a comparative overview of the U.S. and Westminster models of legislative organization and functioning. To strengthen the internal coherence of particular parliamentary committees, IRI invites Romanian MPs to the seminars committee by committee. The program also entails IRI's representative in Bucharest providing advice to MPs about committee structures and urging them to adopt parliamentary rule changes designed to increase the strength of committees.

As with all democracy-related training seminars, it is very difficult to assess the effects of IRI's training seminars on Romanian MPs. Since 1992, Romanian MPs have been the beneficiaries of many training programs—inter-parliamentary exchanges, seminars, conferences, and other activities—many of them sponsored by various European governments and multilateral European organizations. Most Romanian parliamentarians have participated in at least several Western programs; some have become veritable frequent flyers on the circuit of inter-parliamentary exchange.

My interviews with parliamentarians showed that despite the relatively high level of activity in this area since 1992, almost none of the MPs mentioned their participation in training programs; when specifically asked about these programs, they had little—either positive or negative—to say. From their perspective, the training programs seem very small points on the complex horizon of their busy lives as parliamentarians. When they did comment on the programs, it was usually to say that although the information presented by the visiting foreign experts (or by the foreign hosts during foreign visits) was interesting, it was not especially applicable to Romania because the overall socio-political situation in Western countries is so different from that in Romania.

In interviews with members of civic advocacy NGOs and political parties, I received mixed reactions to my inquiry about their perceptions of the value of parliamentary training. Almost all felt that Western donors should at least try to expose parliamentarians to ideas and information about the functioning of parliaments in established democracies. Yet many expressed the view that, for some MPs, the seminars and exchange visits seem to become ends in themselves, serving as distractions from rather than contributions to their regular work.

In general, despite the many Western training programs for Romanian MPs since 1992, there has been little visible improvement in the overall functioning of the Parliament. The major negative characteristics of the Romanian Parliament—low productivity, widespread corruption, and poor public image—have been largely constant over the past several years. It is possible that the training programs have contributed to a gradual process of what might be called the political socialization of Romanian parliamentarians in democratic norms and procedures. It is also possible that, although such a socialization process has not yet had significant effects on the institution of Parliament as a whole, it will be important over the long term. Western donors tend to hold to this idea, although it remains highly conjectural.

A special issue relating to IRI's parliamentary work stems from IRI's status as a partisan political actor in Romania. IRI's parliamentary assistance is intended to be multipartisan, but IRI is well-known in Romanian political circles for its past and present support of the Democratic Convention. As the reaction to IRI's dual role as supporter of the opposition and observer in the 1990 and 1992 elections illustrates, it is problematic for an external actor to try to be simultaneously nonpartisan in one activity and partisan in another. Both IRI and USAID (the main funder of IRI's work in Romania) downplay the possible problems of IRI's ongoing dual role, talking about it as something that the Romanian government has "gotten over." In talking to Romanian officials, however, I found that at least some of them think differently. In the words of one official who works at Parliament:

> The IRI's contribution to Parliament has been zero. Their image [IRI's] cannot be changed here. They are seen and known as the group that supported the opposition. The MPs from the PDSR and other parties close to the government feel they are invited to IRI's seminars to help IRI restore its credibility here. They feel they are being used, and they do not like it.

Some Romanian officials also question IRI's role as an advocate of changes in parliamentary rules regarding committee structure. IRI conceives of and describes this work as technical assistance, but Romanian officials tend to see it as lobbying. They ask why a foreign organization funded by a foreign government has appointed itself to try to change certain rules or procedures in Romania's Parliament. The fact that IRI's work in this area is carried out by an American local representative rather than by a Romanian counterpart organization only puts the issue of foreign meddling in sharper relief.

NGO PARLIAMENTARY PROGRAMS

The other main type of U.S. assistance relating to the Romanian Parliament has been support for certain parliament-related activities of some Romanian NGOs. One such activity has been an effort to increase the "transparency" of the Parliament. This work was initiated by the Romanian Helsinki Committee in early 1993 with funding from the German Marshall Fund of the United States. During 1993, other U.S.-funded Romanian NGOs, such as LADO, as well as the Bucharest office of the USAID-funded International Foundation for Electoral Systems, joined in what became a multifaceted transparency campaign.

These various NGOs had a dual motivation in working to increase the transparency of the Romanian Parliament. In the first place, they intended to lobby the new post-1992 Parliament to advance their agendas on human rights and civic education. Based on their experience with the previous Parliament, they knew that the opaque, secretive methods of operation of the Parliament would render their work difficult. They had a hard time, for example, attempting to obtain copies of draft bills, finding out what committees were dealing with what legislation, or learning the calendar for legislative action. Increasing parliamentary transparency would help facilitate their legislative advocacy efforts, which were crucial to their overall agendas. In addition, these organizations saw the transparency issue as a worthwhile democratization goal: a more transparent Parliament would be more accessible and accountable to all citizens and would be a positive example for other parts of the chronically secretive Romanian government.

After an initial conference for NGOs and parliamentarians on legislative transparency sponsored by the Helsinki Committee in early 1993, various NGOs carried out a series of interrelated activities. These included a petition drive, the establishment of a newsletter on the transparency campaign, and further informational meetings. This work coalesced in early 1994 in a formal request to Parliament by a coalition of Romanian NGOs for the establishment of an NGO information office in the Parliament. The results of this campaign were mixed. Parliament ultimately denied the request for an information office but did take some steps to increase its own transparency, including making draft bills easier to obtain and permitting NGO representatives to attend some committee meetings. Romanian civic advocacy NGOs generally report that the transparency of Parliament has improved since 1992, and both these NGOs and parliamentarians ascribe that change to the transparency campaign. The NGOs acknowledge, however, that the improvements have been very modest and have been relevant primarily to the small circle of NGOs engaged in legislative advocacy.[25]

Another area of Romanian NGO activity aimed at strengthening the Parliament (or, more broadly, strengthening the ideas and principles of political representation in Romania) has been carried out by the Pro Democracy Association (PDA), initially with the primary support of NDI and later with funds from various foreign donors. Since 1992, PDA has organized a series of open meetings in many different parts of the country to bring together Romanian MPs with Romanian citizens. The immediate purpose of these meetings is to permit citizens to pose questions and express opinions directly to their parliamentary representatives. The broader purpose is to strengthen the idea, among both average citizens and parliamentarians, of what political representation in a democracy means and to establish citizen-MP relations as a normal part of Romanian political life.

These meetings do often result in real discussions, which the citizen participants at least sometimes find useful and interesting. MPs differ in their reactions to the gatherings. Some say they value the meetings and have learned something from them about reaching out to voters; others say they go largely because they do not want to be absent when their rivals from other parties are present. Some MPs from Iliescu's party express a dislike for the meetings because they find that the citizens who come are usually persons angry at the government, and that MPs who show up from the PDSR are often singled out for criticism and complaints.

Although these meetings do seem to encourage citizens to talk with MPs, it is unclear whether they have had much effect on changing the general relationship between parliamentarians and the public. Local political analysts report that some MPs are beginning to establish a higher level of communication with constituents, though they cite a number of causes for this trend and do not single out citizen forums as a determining cause. One particular structural feature of Romanian political life, the proportional representation system, is still a large obstacle to any profound change in the distant relationship between parliamentarians and citizens that has prevailed in Romania since 1990. Under this system, the crucial thing for an MP who wants to continue in office is not his popularity in his district, but whether his party includes him on its list of candidates and how high on the list it puts him. Thus MPs tend to worry much more about cultivating good relationships with their party bosses—since those are the persons responsible for the candidate lists—than about developing constituent relations. Without a change in this basic configuration of political incentives, other efforts to change MP-citizen relations are bound to remain a marginal if positive activity.

"BOTTOM-UP" VERSUS "TOP-DOWN" ASSISTANCE

The various U.S. assistance programs relating to the Romanian Parliament underline the basic fact that strengthening parliaments via external assistance is hard work. Parliaments in transitional countries tend to have weak institutional identities. They are often collections of quite disparate individuals with little collective interest in the institution of which they are part. The ground for institutional reform is therefore inevitably weak. Furthermore, parliaments are seldom very interested in reforming themselves. Reform is likely to mean that parliamentarians will have to give up privileges and perquisites. Moreover, parliamentarians are not often prone to acknowledging their own shortcomings or to learning from outside trainers. Yet many parliamentarians enjoy the contacts and exposure that foreign assistance programs involve, so they readily persuade visiting foreign assistance officials of their interest in assistance and go along with proposed assistance programs, at least in form. Even if training programs do positively affect some parliamentarians, the memberships of parliaments in transitional countries tend to turn over relatively rapidly, making it difficult for external actors to have long-term effects on the institutions.

One important point highlighted by the U.S. assistance efforts in Romania is that two distinct methodologies—what might be called the "top-down" and "bottom-up" approaches—exist for parliamentary assistance. In the top-down, conventional model, assistance goes directly to a parliament for training, equipment, information centers, materials, and so on. In the bottom-up model, which is less common and generally more recent, assistance flows to organizations or groups (usually civic advocacy NGOs) within a country to enable them to carry out activities that aim either to change particular aspects of the functioning of a parliament or to shape relations between parliamentarians and citizens.

On the basis of experience in Romania, it seems that in the case of a parliament with serious institutional deficiencies and little apparent inclination toward self-reform, the bottom-up approach may be a better strategy for foreign donors who wish to strengthen the parliament. The actual procedural improvements made as a result of the transparency campaign were modest. Nonetheless, in talking to Romanian MPs it is apparent that they perceive the transparency campaign and transparency itself to be Romanian issues pursued by Romanian organizations. In contrast, the many principles and procedures explained to MPs in the U.S. and European training programs are talked of by Romanian MPs as things outside Romanian culture that foreigners want to see adopted. The prospects for the internalization of new norms in a parliament appear to be greater when those norms are introduced through the bottom-up approach.

CIVIL SOCIETY

A FAVORED CONCEPT

Most Americans involved in promoting democracy in Central and Eastern Europe have a high regard for the concept of civil society. It is an article of faith within much of the U.S. democracy promotion establishment that the rise of civil society was critical to communism's demise in a number of Central and Eastern European countries and that the continued expansion of civil society is crucial to democracy's long-term success in the region. In some other parts of the world, promoting civil society has been a contested and sometimes deliberately neglected element of U.S. democracy assistance. In Latin America, for example, the U.S. government generally avoided "bottom-up" democracy assistance during the 1980s for fear of encouraging populist movements that might be hostile to U.S. anti-communist goals in the region. Civil society promotion in Eastern Europe, however, has been equally popular with conservatives and liberals in the United States. Conservatives are favorably disposed to it because of the association developed in the 1980s between anti-communism and civil society development. For liberals, civil society promotion concords with their general inclination toward a populist "bottom-up" approach rather than an elite-oriented "top-down" approach to democratic development.

"Civil society" is a term used by many people to mean many things.[26] It sometimes refers to the organization of a society on the basis of a certain framework of civic values and sometimes to a particular set or range of institutions, organizations, movements, and associations within a society. The conception of civil society that seems to be most common among Americans working in Eastern Europe (a conception that many in fact learned from Eastern European intellectuals) is a version of the latter type. According to this definition, civil society is understood to be "an intermediate associational realm between state and family populated by organizations which are separate from the state, enjoy autonomy in relation to the state and are formed voluntarily by members of society to protect or extend their interests or values."[27] Civil society is considered to function as a two-way channel between citizens and the state, serving both to mobilize and articulate the interests of citizens and to hold the state more accountable and render it more responsive.

Although this conception of civil society is relatively broad, U.S. government assistance programs in Central and Eastern Europe that explicitly aim to "promote civil society" have tended to be more narrowly focused. Such assistance has been concentrated on what I will here call civic advocacy organizations—small, nonprofit NGOs seeking to affect governmental policy. Up to 1995, U.S. civil society assistance concentrated on the more political types of such NGOs, generally those dealing with human rights, ethnic conflict, and civic education. With the recent establishment of the Democracy Network program, socio-economic NGOs now also fall within the U.S. civil-society assistance effort—provided they are policy-oriented NGOs, not merely organizations that seek to resolve individuals' problems with no effort to change governmental policy (although non-policy-oriented economic and social welfare NGOs are often recipients of U.S. support from the economic and humanitarian rather than the democracy components of the overall U.S. assistance portfolio). The U.S. conception of civil society not only leaves out non-policy-oriented NGOs; it also excludes other types of non-state actors, such as religious organizations, ethnic associations, sports clubs, nature societies, cultural associations, and others. Recently, USAID has begun to use the term "civil society organization" for the type of NGO that it makes the focus of its civil society work. This highlights the way USAID tends to narrow its interpretation of the concept of civil society not just to NGOs, but to one particular category of NGOs.

CIVIL SOCIETY IN ROMANIA

Unlike most other communist countries in Central and Eastern Europe, Romania did not enjoy an emerging civil society in the 1980s. The Ceauşescu regime was devastatingly absolutist, permitting no organized socio-political activity outside the rigid framework of state control. After December 1989, there was an initial burst of associational life in Romania as many people reacted to the sudden political opening by forming organizations of all types. This initial florescence had two important characteristics. First, many of the new organizations were not serious initiatives but passing enthusiasms. Second, the major NGOs concerned with civil and political issues that formed early on were generally fairly closely linked—either in spirit or more directly—to the political opposition. This was an inevitable consequence of the fact that, in the immediate aftermath of 1989 in Romania, the concepts of political opposition and political independence overlapped considerably. In the first stage of transition away from a completely state-dominated system of power, any group that asserted genuine independence from the state was in a sense a form of political opposition.

The profile of associational life in Romania has evolved since that early period. The initial burst of enthusiasm for forming organizations has faded, and many of the first groups formed no longer exist, or exist only on paper. New organizations are being established, though at a steadier and more measured rate. These entities are still generally small and their existence is precarious, but in many cases they are more serious ventures with more consequential long-term prospects than before. Moreover, the link between civic advocacy NGOs and the opposition parties is no longer as close or common as it was. Some NGOs remain associated with the political opposition, but many do not. A number of the civic advocacy organizations, for example, pursue their agendas quite separately from the opposition. They work cooperatively with the government when they believe it necessary, or criticize the opposition on particular issues. And they measure themselves by the level of their professionalism rather than by the fervency of their opposition.

THE U.S. ASSISTANCE

The principal types of civic advocacy organizations that the United States has supported in Romania have been human rights groups, civic education organizations, and environmental groups.

This section focuses on human rights and civic education groups. Environmental NGOs have been an important (and successful) area of U.S. assistance in Romania, but environmental work has not been categorized as democracy assistance and has only recently begun to be thought of as such.

Almost all of the major human rights organizations in Romania, including the Romanian Helsinki Committee, the Romanian Society for Human Rights (SIRDO), the League for the Defense of Human Rights (LADO), *Liga Pro-Europa*, and the Association of Lawyers in Defense of Human Rights (APADO), have received U.S. support. This support has come from various USAID-funded and NED-funded intermediary organizations, particularly the Institute for Democracy in Eastern Europe, as well as from the German Marshall Fund and the Soros Foundations. This support has consisted in part of technical assistance—in particular, in-country advice and assistance by long-term advisors sent to Romania by the Washington-based International Human Rights Law Group. Unlike most other U.S. democracy assistance programs, the support has also involved direct grants to the Romanian organizations. Like the human rights organizations to which they have been channeled, these direct grants have been small—usually in the range of $10,000 to $50,000.

The United States has also supported various civic education efforts in Romania. By far the most substantial such support has been the assistance provided by NDI to the Pro Democracy Association (PDA). As discussed in more detail below, NDI provided most of the operating funds for the first several years of PDA's existence, as well as extensive technical assistance and much general institutional support.

The United States has not only supported particular civic advocacy NGOs but also attempted to foster general consciousness-raising about NGOs within Romanian political society. The main such effort was the Civic Voice program carried out by the International Foundation for Electoral Systems from 1993 to 1995. Under this program, IFES organized several major conferences to bring together Romanian NGO representatives, relevant Romanian officials, and foreign experts, and provided institutional support to nascent NGOs in different parts of the country.

EFFECTS

The effects of this varied assistance can be assessed by focusing first on the effects of the assistance on the Romanian organizations and, second, on the effects of the Romanian organizations on Romanian society. The U.S. assistance, including that of the German Marshall Fund and the Soros Foundations, to the Romanian human rights organizations and to at least some of the civic education organizations (in particular the Pro Democracy Association) has been very important, even essential, to their existence. These organizations depend almost entirely on foreign funding (the issue of sustainability is discussed separately below), and the U.S. assistance has been a major part of such funding (the Dutch government has been the other major funder of human rights groups in Romania).

Persons within these organizations report that the U.S. training and technical assistance was very useful when they were getting under way. Such assistance helped them learn what human rights advocacy and civic education consist of, how advocacy organizations are run, and, more generally, how to operate as a non-state actor in a new democracy. This assistance appears to have been more valued than much of the training and advice in other areas of U.S. democracy assistance because it was carried out primarily by a few advisors working in-country in a sustained fashion rather than by short-term visiting experts presenting materials at occasional seminars. Nonetheless, members of relatively well-established Romanian NGOs feel that the value of such technical advice has diminished substantially now that the organizations are on their feet and moving ahead.

Some Romanian NGO representatives emphasize that above and beyond the financial support and technical assistance that U.S. organizations have provided, a key aspect of the U.S. role was the psychological impact of the early, high-visibility importance that Americans attached to NGO development in Romania. One Romanian NGO activist put it as follows:

> Suddenly in 1990 there were all sorts of Americans in Romania talking about NGOs all the time, something most of us had never even heard of, and the Americans were from NGOs, with all sorts of letter names: NDI, IRI, IFES, FTUI. As a result, people around here began taking this NGO thing seriously.

The impact of human rights and civic education NGOs on Romanian society has been valuable, albeit modest. The human rights groups have inserted human rights concepts and concerns into the language and the thinking of the growing Romanian political society. They have forced the government at least to give more consideration to certain basic rights, such as free speech and due process, and to recognize publicly (although not always to believe privately) that oppositional politics and human rights advocacy are not the same. The Romanian Helsinki Committee has successfully lobbied to produce positive changes from a human rights viewpoint in various laws enacted since 1992, including the criminal code, the law on public assembly, and the law on religion in schools. SIRDO has conveyed information and materials on teaching human rights to many school teachers in different parts of the country. Various human rights organizations have contributed to positive resolutions of cases involving police abuse of citizens.

The Pro Democracy Association has helped establish among Romanian political elites the idea of non-partisan, pro-democratic civic education as a valid and necessary activity—a genuine accomplishment, given the polarized nature of Romanian political life and the serious lack of any tradition of democratic civic education. PDA has also helped increase the understanding of democratic political processes on the part of some Romanian citizens and brought some parliamentarians into closer contact with the public, although, as noted in the previous section, changing the overall weak quality of political representation in Romania will require deeper structural changes. IFES's "Civic Voice" program helped increase communication among Romanian NGOs and fostered a growing sense of a coherent NGO community in Romania. It also managed to get technical assistance to small NGOs far from Bucharest, which are not reached by most other foreign assistance providers. The IFES program also helped advance a still-tentative process of positive evolution with regard to the Romanian government's attitude and policies toward NGOs. Many Romanian officials remain suspicious of and even hostile to the idea of NGOs, which they see as a potential threat to the government's power. But in part because of the IFES program and some efforts sponsored by the Soros Foundations and some European donors aimed directly at the issue of government policy toward NGOs, Romanian officials have begun to understand NGOs better and to accept their role in Romanian society.

These various contributions of Romanian human rights and civic education NGOs are certainly worthwhile, but they also represent a quite limited impact overall. They have had most effect within relatively limited circles of people—politicians, journalists, intellectuals, and civic activists—primarily in Bucharest and in a few other major cities. The general level of human rights awareness and democratic civic consciousness in Romania remains low. The positive effects have been much less dramatic than many of the people involved—foreign providers of assistance and Romanian civic activists alike—initially hoped for and expected. The experience of Romanian civic advocacy organizations has had the somewhat paradoxical effect of, on the one hand, empowering a number of genuinely talented and dynamic civic activists, transforming their own sense of self and their place in society—while, on the other hand, creating a sense of discouragement among many of these people as to what it will take to change, both more broadly and more deeply, the stunted civic consciousness of most Romanians.

SUSTAINABILITY AND AUTHENTICITY

The U.S. assistance to civic advocacy NGOs in Romania raises numerous questions about foreign support for civil society development beyond the simpler issue of what effects the new NGOs are having on their society. Two questions that arise in Romania, and generally throughout the region, relate to the sustainability and the authenticity of foreign-supported NGOs.

The question of whether and how the many new NGOs in Eastern Europe can find means of financial support other than Western funding becomes increasingly pressing as the number of NGOs continues to multiply and the duration of Western assistance grows increasingly uncertain. In Romania, the level of dependence of many NGOs on foreign funding is very high. When the director of a Romanian NGO talks about diversifying funding sources, he or she is usually speaking about shifting from one principal foreign donor to a mix of foreign donors. Membership contributions and domestic corporate sponsorship are currently not feasible options as principal funding sources in Romania, though some NGO activists believe that corporate donations can be developed significantly in coming years. Government funding to NGOs, an arrangement common in some Western European countries, is shunned as an option by most Romanian NGO activists who, probably with reason, believe that the Romanian government would not allow them to maintain their operational independence if it gave them funds. In short, at this point the new civic advocacy NGO sector in Romania is largely unsustainable without continued foreign funding.

Most of the U.S. organizations that have been assisting Romanian NGOs have not given much attention to the issue of sustainability.[28] This is in part because they have been working in Romania with a short-term perspective. They rushed in after Ceauşescu's fall and hurriedly threw together programs to help Romania keep moving in a democratic direction. They have conceived of their work in Romania as part of a transitional phase and have not focused much on long-term issues of any sort, including sustainability. The lack of attention to sustainability is also due to the fact that the U.S. organizations do not actually have any solution to the problem. As a result, they tend psychologically to assign the problem to their Romanian grantees. Their implicit, and sometimes explicit, attitude is "we have helped them get going; they will have to figure out how to continue." This attitude tends to surface only when the U.S. organizations begin to contemplate cutting off their funding to local NGOs, producing confusion and often resentment among Romanian NGO activists who feel taken by surprise and let down harshly.

The second issue concerning foreign support for NGO development is that of authenticity—an issue with a long history in Western assistance to the developing world. With Romanian NGOs, the issue can be posed succinctly as follows: Does the fact that many Romanian NGOs are almost entirely dependent upon foreign funding mean that they are not authentic organizations but foreign implants with no genuine relation to Romanian culture? The issue is posed particularly vividly by the Pro Democracy Association because of the extremely close relationship it had with NDI during its first several years of existence. NDI did not simply fund PDA; it was closely involved in every step of the organization's development. This aid far exceeded the support received by any other Romanian civic advocacy organization. When NDI began working in Romania in 1990, it had previously helped establish local civic education and election monitoring groups in other transitional countries. After the May 1990 elections, NDI concluded that there was a need for such an organization in Romania. NDI representatives brought together the people who initially formed PDA, gave them extensive advice and ideas about what sorts of activities would be useful (such as election monitoring and voter education), provided start-up as well as operational funds for the first several years, placed a succession of NDI representatives in Bucharest for several years to work full-time with PDA, and sent Washington staff to Romania frequently to oversee the work and provide additional guidance.

In Romania, one hears two views about PDA, representing the two traditional poles of debate in aid-recipient countries about

71

the authenticity of foreign-supported local organizations. One view that surfaces both within the government and, interestingly, in parts of the NGO sector, holds PDA to be an inauthentic foreign transplant. Among some government officials, this view is just part of a larger hostility toward NGOs generally, and toward foreign support for NGOs. Those in the NGO sector who view PDA in this way—primarily persons in some of the human rights organizations—seem to believe that NDI's support crossed some line between merely backing an organization and actually creating an organization. They feel that PDA's agenda of voter education is an American idea with no resonance in Romania, and that PDA has traded heavily on its U.S. backing in ways that inevitably brand it as a foreign transplant.

The other view, which one hears in much of the broader NGO community and more generally among Romanians who are aware of PDA, is that although PDA started with a strong American coloring, over time it has established itself as a legitimate Romanian organization because Romanians carry out the work and run the organization. The fact that PDA's agenda was clearly taken from its foreign sponsor, at least initially, and that activities such as voter education and election monitoring have no tradition in Romania, does not in this view render PDA inauthentic. "At least they are doing something," is a common sentiment expressed about PDA in Romania. Or, as several people in Bucharest said to me, given that Romania's political history is not very democratic, every Romanian organization working to promote democracy can be dismissed as inauthentic in some way—and such an argument would condemn Romania to live in its undemocratic past.

SOME UNDERLYING ASSUMPTIONS

Many Americans involved in democracy assistance in Romania, and in Central and Eastern Europe generally, translate the very general goal of promoting civil society into the quite specific approach of assisting civic advocacy NGOs. Without seeking to refute this approach, it is nonetheless worthwhile to highlight how particularly American it is, and to identify some of the embedded assumptions that make it so. The basic assumption of this approach is that civic advocacy NGOs—in contrast to (for example) service-sector NGOs or other types of non-state actors, such as churches or social movements—are the core of civil society. This assumption clearly reflects a certain slice of the U.S. domestic experience.

The United States is heavily populated by NGO advocacy groups seeking to influence the national, state, and local governments. The extraordinary number and range of civic advocacy groups is a form of civil society development particular to, or at least most extensively elaborated in, the United States. Many Americans who seek to promote civil society in Central and Eastern Europe come out of the U.S. NGO world and instinctively try to reproduce it abroad.

A second, related assumption in the U.S. approach to civil society promotion in the region is a belief in the central importance of legislative advocacy as a tool of socio-political change. Many U.S. assistance organizations working with Romanian NGOs hold out the ability to effect legislative change as the *sine qua non* of successful NGO work. Other methods of exerting pressure for socio-political change, such as social mobilization, civil disobedience, or popular demonstrations, are rarely mentioned in U.S. civil society assistance programs abroad. Again, this assumption clearly stems from U.S. experience, or rather the experience of the sorts of U.S. NGOs that work in Central and Eastern Europe promoting civil society. For these NGOs, America is a society of laws. To change the society, one changes the laws—in a technocratic, gradualistic fashion. An additional component of this assumption is the belief that it is normal for legislatures to be highly penetrated and influenced by organized special-interest groups. Foreign parliaments that resist such penetration are perceived as undemocratic and in need of modification.

A third assumption of the U.S. approach is that the engine of civil society development in Central and Eastern Europe will be NGOs pursuing broad public-interest agendas—such as human rights, civic education, and the environment—rather than informal groups of citizens pursuing relatively specific self-interest agendas—such as ameliorating a financial wrong done by the government to a certain group of people, getting permission to expand an open-air market in a certain sector of a city, or persuading the government to extend a railroad line to an unserved area. Broad public-interest agendas appeal to U.S. donors; they have a noble, altruistic quality, and they promise impact on many members of the society.

Yet while public-interest advocacy may be important in the United States, in a transitional society such as Romania, civil society development is more likely to be fueled by people working together to advance their immediate collective self-interest. Thanks to the efforts of U.S. and European donors, there does now exist a thin, somewhat precariously established layer of public-interest NGOs in Romania. If one talks to mayors and other local officials around the country about their contacts with citizens, however, they report that the groups they notice most are the small groups of citizens who increasingly come to see them about issues of current concern—tenant associations seeking to resolve problems with their apartment buildings, farmers' groups trying to work out land problems, and groups of local entrepreneurs seeking to open new types of businesses. These groups are pursuing their narrow, collective self-interest—not any broader public interest.

It is this type of associational life, or civil society development, that is directly relevant to the largest number of Romanians and is growing most rapidly in Romania. Assistance to these types of associations does not, however, easily match the public-interest emphasis of the U.S. programs to promote civil society. Even when U.S. organizations go to the local level to foster NGOs, they tend to try to form or assist groups of citizens to work on behalf of the local community generally rather than on those groups' own particular interests. The habitual U.S. emphasis of U.S. democracy promoters on public interest advocacy is understandable in U.S. terms, but in a society where most people are struggling just to get by, it is much more difficult to mobilize individuals to work for some generalized public good than for their immediate self-interest.

TRADE UNIONS

A LONG HISTORY

Assisting the development of trade unions is one of the oldest forms of U.S. foreign assistance. The AFL-CIO has been engaged in such work from the beginning of this century, with significant U.S. government support since the 1940s. The rationale for this work has varied over time, usually in conformity with the changing overall emphasis of U.S. foreign policy. In the 1920s and 1930s, AFL-CIO support for unions in Latin America was linked to the general U.S. interest in reducing the nationalization of U.S. businesses. During World War II, the AFL-CIO highlighted antifascist objectives in its work abroad. Throughout the Cold War, the AFL-CIO made anti-communism the dominant rationale of its international work. When in the second half of the 1980s U.S.

foreign policy began moving away from anti-communism toward a greater concern for democracy promotion *per se*, the importance of independent trade unions for the development of democracy emerged as a major theme of the AFL-CIO's work abroad.[29]

With funding from both USAID and the National Endowment for Democracy, AFL-CIO assistance to foreign unions has been an important component of U.S. democracy assistance efforts in recent years. In Eastern Europe prior to 1989, the AFL-CIO, working through its affiliate, the Free Trade Union Institute (FTUI), primarily worked with Solidarity in Poland. After 1989, FTUI developed programs in all of the region's countries. In Romania, FTUI became involved almost immediately after the fall of Ceauşescu and continues to be engaged there today.

THE COMPLEX WORLD OF ROMANIAN UNIONS

During the communist years, unions in Romania—as elsewhere throughout the Soviet bloc—were an extension of the state apparatus and organized under a single federation, the General Trade Union Federation of Romania. A few strikes and other labor disturbances did erupt during the 1970s and 1980s, but these were the actions of particular groups of workers, not of unions *per se*. Since December 1989, this formerly monolithic, state-dominated world of unions has given way to a varied, often confusing mix of independent, partially independent, and still state-dominated unions, union federations, and confederations.[30]

Immediately after the overthrow of Ceauşescu, the General Trade Union Federation began to metamorphose into a new entity, the Confederation of Free Trade Unions of Romania (CNSLR), which initially at least seemed to have close ties with the new ruling powers. At the same time, new, independent unions began to form, and a confederation of independent unions, the Independent Trade Union Confederation *Frăţia* was established in January 1990. In June 1990, a second major confederation of independent unions, the Alfa Cartel, was formed. In this rapidly changing union environment, many state-dominated unions continued to exist, some with close ties to the most retrograde elements of the power structure. This fact was vividly demonstrated by the ability of the government to activate the miners' unions to crush the University Square demonstration in June 1990.

75

Since 1990, the political evolution of the major union confederations has been exceedingly complex and often quite unexpected. The two main confederations and their leaders, for example, have taken diametrically opposed paths. The leader of CNSLR, Victor Ciorbea, originally viewed in the West as a pro-government flack, led CNSLR steadily away from the government into a merger with *Frăţia* in 1993; in late 1994, he broke away from the merged CNSLR-*Frăţia* to form his own confederation, which is openly pro-opposition. In contrast, the leader of *Frăţia*, Miron Mitrea, originally hailed in the West as the first truly independent union leader, led *Frăţia* into a progressively closer relationship with the government. He left *Frăţia*-CNSLR in late 1994 and now pursues political ambitions within Iliescu's party.

In general, CNSLR, *Frăţia*, and the Alfa Cartel, which during most of the 1990-95 period together represented the large majority of union members in Romania, have attempted to achieve some unity of action in the face of a constant government policy of attempting to divide and co-opt the unions. This striving for unity has produced some results in terms of concerted action to obtain wage hikes and other concessions from the government, but the power of the unions remains less strong than hoped for by many in the union movement. The government's ability to co-opt unions has been facilitated by the slow process of economic reform, which has left many Romanians employees of state enterprises.

The union confederations have had to do battle not only with a powerful, resourceful government but also with their own shortcomings. The leaders of the major confederations and federations have engaged in constant in-fighting over control of the union patrimony left from the communist years, as well as over their own grand personal ambitions and rivalries. The weakness and divisiveness of the opposition parties have contributed to the divisions within the union leadership—and to the tendency of some union leaders to pursue a politically two-sided approach, combining formal pro-opposition positioning with back-door special relationships with the government.

FTUI'S PROGRAM

FTUI's work in Romania falls into two distinct phases, though it has been in the service of a single goal: helping to foster trade unions that are genuinely independent of the Romanian government. In the first phase, from 1990 to early 1992, FTUI worked actively to support *Frăţia*. Like many in that period, FTUI saw *Frăţia* and its leader, Miron Mitrea, as the bright future of independent trade unions in Romania. FTUI quickly developed a close, support-ive relationship with *Frăţia*. Representatives of FTUI and the AFL-CIO visited Bucharest frequently to express their support for *Frăţia*, give speeches for *Frăţia* members, and provide advice and guidance to *Frăţia*'s leaders. FTUI quickly provided *Frăţia* with over $100,000 in equipment and supplies, including computers, copying machines, fax machines, printers, and newsprint. FTUI also initiated training sessions for *Frăţia* members on union-building methods. FTUI's goal was not merely to help *Frăţia* expand; it wanted to make *Frăţia* the dominant and, if possible, the only labor confederation in Romania.

But FTUI's relationship with *Frăţia* fell apart almost as quickly as it had been put together. As early as December 1990, at the time of the first general strike, FTUI representatives began to have doubts as to whether Miron Mitrea really wanted *Frăţia* to be inde-pendent of the government. By mid-1991, FTUI believed Mitrea was seeking some sort of collaborative relationship with the govern-ment. FTUI warned Mitrea in late 1991 of its concerns on this issue, but Mitrea did not respond positively. FTUI consequently terminated its special relationship with *Frăţia* in the first half of 1992.[31]

After its disappointing experience with *Frăţia*, FTUI in 1992 embarked on a new phase of work in Romania consisting of two lines of activity. First, it began organizing training seminars for union leaders and activists on union-building; these sessions were open to persons from unions in all of the major confederations. Second, together with a British electrical union, FTUI started provid-ing assistance—training, advice, equipment—to the National Union Bloc (BNS), a new confederation of independent unions formed in 1991. In reaction to its experience with *Frăţia*, FTUI has developed its relationship with BNS cautiously, building up the assistance slowly as it becomes persuaded that BNS definitely intends to stay independent of the Romanian government.

As much as any other U.S. organization working in Romania, FTUI holds to the black-and-white view of post-1989 Romanian political life, perceiving the country as starkly divided between entrenched neo-communists and struggling democratic forces. This is how FTUI initially saw the emergent post-1989 union scene: *Frăţia* was the heroic voice of the new spirit of independent union-ism; CNSLR was no more than a newly labeled version of the old communist confederation; and the Alfa Cartel, not being linked to *Frăţia*, was suspect. This initial view was quickly undermined by events, and the world of trade unions has since 1990 proven to be one defined by shades of gray, with the categories of independent and government-dominated unions constantly intermixed and blurred. Yet FTUI has responded not by changing its underlying black-and-white view but only by changing local partners. Disappointed by *Frăţia*, FTUI looked for another confederation that it believed was genuinely independent to become its primary partner in Romania. Despite the frequently ambiguous relations of Romanian unions to the government, FTUI representatives continue to describe unions in Romania as having only two modes of being— independent or co-opted. FTUI continues to conceive of its role as helping independent unions to develop and to learn to resist the power and influence of the government.

EFFECTS

FTUI's intensive assistance to *Frăţia* in 1990 and 1991 helped *Frăţia* expand its membership and strengthen its internal organization. It also gave *Frăţia* a strong boost in terms of its general visibility and position within Romanian political life. A 1993 NED-sponsored evaluation of FTUI support for *Frăţia* highlighted this latter point: "As the only union designated for assistance in the early days after the revolution, *Frăţia* received the mantle of external acceptance from FTUI. Being anointed with the western seal of approval gave it enormous prestige and clout in Romania."[32] Unfortunately, however, although FTUI helped strengthen *Frăţia*, this strengthening turned out to not serve FTUI's objective of building *Frăţia* into a dominant, independent trade union. Miron Mitrea used FTUI's assistance, and the aid he received from other Western labor organizations, to advance his own quite different agenda, maximizing his personal power and establishing *Frăţia* as the dominant but by no means genuinely independent union confederation.

The effects of FTUI's assistance in the second phase of its involvement in Romania have been more straightforward. Its training seminars have contributed to greater understanding among union activists of basic aspects of U.S. practice with respect to union organization, collective bargaining, and other features of labor relations. These seminars are one part of a larger flow of labor-related information being conveyed to Romanian unions by various international labor federations and foreign unions. FTUI's assistance to the National Union Bloc has been helping that confederation strengthen its internal organization. FTUI's general training seminars and its assistance to BNS are, however, relatively modest in scale and unlikely to have more than modest effects—as evidenced by the fact that the overall strength of the unions in Romania has not changed significantly in recent years, despite the international assistance they have received.

PARTISANSHIP REVISITED AND OTHER ISSUES

FTUI's work in Romania raises important broader issues concerning democracy assistance. First, the group's ardent early embrace of *Frăţia* highlights the fact that backing a favorite in a field of competing actors in a highly fluid political situation—instead of offering ideas and knowledge to all actors within a sector—is a risky business. Favorites can go badly astray, often in very unexpected ways. When they do, moreover, assistance that has strengthened them can end up helping them achieve objectives quite different from those contemplated by the donors. Even a close relationship between a powerful foreign assistance organization and a fledgling local recipient usually gives the assistance organization much less influence over the recipient than the donor tends to imagine.

Backing favorites is also likely to generate hostility among other local actors in the field—hostility not easily dissipated, even if a less partisan approach is later adopted. FTUI's aggressive championing of *Frăţia* early on, combined with FTUI's negative, often dismissive attitude toward other labor confederations, alienated many unionists in Romania. In my interviews with them, union officials in Romania emphasized that, despite political differences and infighting, activists in the various union federations and confederations are personally and professionally entwined in many ways; it was harmful, as well as unpopular, they feel, for FTUI to have come on the scene drawing sharp lines between the groups and encouraging union leaders to do the same. Even though FTUI has since 1992 adopted a somewhat less partisan approach, the impression of FTUI as a partisan, divisive actor in Romania still lingers among at least some Romanian unionists. FTUI's growing relationship with BNS also makes some unionists believe that FTUI is once again trying to anoint a favorite.

A second general issue raised by FTUI's work in Romania is the compatibility of union-building assistance with other U.S.

policies and programs in the country. In Romania as elsewhere in the region, the U.S. government is funding union-building activities in Romania even as it is urging the Romanian government to undertake economic restructuring—which, if pursued seriously, will entail closing down state factories and putting many people out of work, at least for the short term. It may be, as FTUI representatives argue when asked about this issue, that stronger, more independent unions will facilitate economic restructuring because they will understand that privatization and restructuring is in the workers' long-term interest. But it may well be that strong, more independent unions will provide stronger resistance to the closing of factories and to the strict wage targets called for in stabilization and restructuring programs.

What is striking is how little attention seems to be paid to this issue of cross-program consistency within U.S. assistance planning circles. FTUI basically sets its agenda, gets its funds, and carries out its programs largely on its own. The other parts of the U.S. assistance program do the same. As long as each activity can be justified individually as in some way supporting democratization or economic liberalization, all are assumed to be mutually compatible.

A third general issue concerning FTUI's work has been highlighted by some Western European unionists working in Romania and some Romanian unionists who question why the AFL-CIO is working in Romania or Eastern Europe at all. They point out that the U.S. labor movement has fared very poorly within the United States in recent decades, and they question whether the AFL-CIO has much credibility in touting itself internationally as an effective labor movement. They also question the appropriateness for Romania and other Eastern European countries of the U.S. model of union development and labor relations implicit in FTUI's work— the model of unions organizing company by company in a hostile environment of anti-union bosses. They argue that such countries are on the track to a more continental model of labor relations involving business-labor partnerships and collaborative relationships with governments.

THE MEDIA

PROMOTING INDEPENDENT MEDIA

Clearly Americans attach tremendous importance to the electronic and print media, which within American society are viewed as fulfilling two functions crucial to democracy. The media serve as a check on governmental power—that is, they are a primary means of ensuring accountability and transparency of governmental action. The media also keep citizens informed about what is going on within the society; they provide a sort of informational glue that helps hold together a large, heterogeneous population. Given the centrality of the media in contemporary American society, it is almost inevitable that Americans who go abroad to promote democracy will make media development one of their priorities. As U.S. democracy assistance has expanded over the past ten years, media assistance—programs to train journalists, various forms of support for newspapers, radio, and television, funding of media-watch organizations—has been a growing activity. USIA has been heavily involved in this field, particularly on the educational side. USAID and NED have also been actively engaged.

U.S. media assistance generally emphasizes two key principles: that media should maintain strict independence from government in determining the content of their publishing and broadcasting, and that media should strive toward professionalism and non-partisanship, clearly separating fact from opinion and pursuing a high degree of factual accuracy. Because private ownership is a cardinal feature of the U.S. media, the private ownership model is often explicitly and implicitly part of U.S. media assistance programs abroad. This is true for radio and television as much as for newspapers, even though the U.S. model of primarily private ownership of radio and television is not widely shared in other established Western democracies.

THE EVOLUTION OF THE MEDIA IN ROMANIA SINCE 1989

Rigid state control of all forms of public information and communication was an essential feature of the communist system in Romania. Ceaușescu reduced Romanian television, radio, and newspapers to slavish propaganda tools of the government. Access to even the most basic communication and information equipment was restricted—typewriters had to be registered with the police, copying machines were scarce, printing presses were strictly controlled, and personal computers were almost nonexistent. Access to foreign sources of information was available only to a very small circle of party loyalists, with the singular exception of foreign radio broadcasts, such as those of the BBC and Radio Free Europe, which did get through to many people.

Since 1989, the situation of the media in Romania has changed dramatically for the better, although it still falls short of Western democratic standards. Television, by far the most influential journalistic medium in Romania, has made the least progress in terms of moving away from the past. More than five years after the fall of Ceauşescu, there is still only one national television station, the state channel TVR1, and its news broadcasts closely follow the government line. President Iliescu, highly aware of the powerful influence that TVR1 has on the political outlook of Romanians, especially in the countryside, has strongly resisted external and internal pressures to lessen the government's grip on TVR1. Local private television stations have been established to serve Bucharest and most provincial cities. These stations are independent of the government, although they are in some cases owned by businessmen with close ties to the ruling circles; on the whole, however, they are much less influential than TVR1. Cable television is growing very rapidly in Romania, particularly in the cities, bringing foreign news and entertainment shows to a large and growing number of households.[33]

The few national radio stations are all state-run, and the main such station, *România-Actualităţi*, has a dominant audience share. Yet the news broadcasts on *România-Actualităţi* are less pro-government than those on state television. In general, radio plays a much less important role than television in shaping Romanian public opinion. Local private radio stations have sprung up in great numbers, and they are providing a range of programming quite different from the state stations, including a wider range of news subjects and relatively open-ended talk shows. Foreign radio stations are still listened to by some Romanians, but they no longer have the impact they had in the pre-1989 period.

A wide variety of newspapers and opinion journals is now published in Romania, and the press faces very few formal restrictions on what it can print. Although there are many newspapers, their total circulation is not that large; in a recent survey, only 8 percent of Romanians cited newspapers as their main source of information about political life (compared to 59 percent for television and 17 percent for radio).[34] Three daily newspapers have established significant national circulations. The largest of these, *Evenimentul Zilei*, follows no clear political line. The other two, *Adevărul* and *România Liberă*, are (respectively) somewhat independent and fervently pro-opposition. Local newspapers have become increasingly important. Many practical obstacles, some of which are the responsibility of the government, still limit the publication and distribution of newspapers. For example, there is still only one factory for newsprint in Romania, resulting in frequent shortages (foreign newsprint being prohibitively expensive due to high import duties). Printing presses are also still few in number, with certain papers favored at the state presses and most papers unable to afford the high cost of importing a press from abroad.

ASSISTANCE TO ROMANIAN MEDIA

Prior to 1989, what limited democracy assistance the United States was able to sponsor in Eastern Europe often related to the media; it involved support for newsletters, underground newspapers, émigré magazines, and radio broadcasting. Since 1989, media assistance has been a major part of the U.S. democracy assistance portfolio in every country in the region. USIA has been involved in many media-related projects, and the USAID-funded International Media Fund—a Washington-based organization established in 1990 specifically to promote independent media in Eastern Europe (and later the former Soviet Union)—was a principal actor until it was disbanded in 1995.

In Romania, the International Media Fund received more USAID support than any other U.S. organization involved in democracy assistance for the 1990-94 period as a whole. Two main projects have dominated U.S. aid to the media in Romania. In 1990, the U.S. government underwrote the purchase of a printing press (costing approximately $350,000) and provided newsprint and other supplies for the newspaper *România Liberă*. Between 1990 and 1993, the International Media Fund (with USAID funding of approximately $800,000) helped *România Liberă* get the press properly housed and put in working order. The second major media project was support for SOTI, the first private television station in Romania. From 1990 to 1993, the International Media Fund spent between $500,000 and $1,000,000 of U.S. government funds providing extensive technical support to SOTI.

USAID, NED, and USIA have also sponsored a variety of smaller media-related projects in Romania. In 1990, Northeastern University carried out a project to create private local radio stations—an effort that made a lasting impression on many Romanians both because it was one of the very first U.S. assistance projects under way after December 1989 and because of the freewheeling

83

manner in which it was implemented. From 1993 to 1995, the International Media Fund sponsored training courses for television and radio journalists in Romania. The Institute for Democracy in Eastern Europe, primarily with NED funding, has given many small grants (usually well under $20,000) to small independent journals and magazines. The NED has also recently been funding a small media-watch group that seeks to improve the standards of the Romanian press.

All of the U.S. media projects in Romania, large and small, have the same general objective of fostering the growth of independent media. The analysis here will focus on the two large projects: the assistance to *România Liberă* and SOTI.

ROMÂNIA LIBERĂ AND THE U.S. CONCEPT OF INDEPENDENT MEDIA

The U.S. assistance to *România Liberă* was clearly useful to that newspaper. Receiving a large printing press was a major benefit, allowing *România Liberă* to expand its circulation and to circumvent the problems that most newspapers face in having to rely on the overburdened state printing facilities. U.S. assistance helped *România Liberă* consolidate its position as by far the most widely circulated pro-opposition newspaper. The U.S. assistance has thus helped make a newspaper with a pro-opposition perspective available to a significant number of Romanians; *România Liberă* is the only pro-opposition newspaper that has established a national distribution network reaching beyond Bucharest and a few other major cities.

The answer to whether the U.S. assistance to *România Liberă* has helped foster the growth of independent media in Romania depends on how one defines independent media. The U.S. government talks a great deal in Romania (and in many other countries) about supporting the growth of independent media without clarifying a basic ambiguity about the intended meaning of the term "independent." On the one hand, "independent media" may refer to media not controlled or heavily influenced by the government of the country in which they operate. On the other hand, it may mean media that are neither closely affiliated with any one political party nor overtly partisan in any way. *România Liberă* is an independent newspaper in the former sense but not in the latter. It is a fiercely partisan paper following an adamant anti-Iliescu, pro-opposition line. The insistence of the U.S. government on referring to its support for *România Liberă* as support for "independent media" confused and angered Romanian government officials in the early 1990s. They felt that such assistance was another example of the United States using politically non-partisan concepts like "independent" as a cover for highly partisan involvement.

The U.S. assistance to *România Liberă* has failed to contribute to the development of independent media in the full sense of the term (i.e., non-partisan rather than simply not government-controlled). It also has not contributed to the development of professionalized media. *România Liberă* is a bold newspaper, but it is not a very good one. It is held in low regard not only by people unsympathetic to its political line but also by many opposition supporters. This negative rating stems from *România Liberă*'s tendentiousness, its tendency to value opinion over facts, and the paper's low reporting standards. The quality of the newspaper has not improved over time; if anything, it has been decreasing. For USAID in the early 1990s, however, the quality of the newspaper was not a central issue. The U.S. government was determined to support a national newspaper willing to challenge the government's line. It hoped over the long term to see the development in Romania of non-partisan, professionalized media, but in its desire to help break the government's monopoly on sources of information, it was willing to settle for much less in the short term.

THE SOTI FIASCO

In early 1990, a small group of Romanians, primarily intellectuals within the emerging opposition ranks, began thinking and talking about the possibility of launching a private television station to break the government's monopoly in that medium. U.S. assistance officials and policy-makers heard about the initiative and took up its cause, pressuring President Iliescu to permit the establishment of at least one private television station. The issue was elevated by the State Department in 1990 as a key test of Iliescu's democratic intentions (although there was debate on this point within the U.S. government, with those U.S. officials who were more sympathetic to the Romanian government arguing that insistence on the establishment of private television represented the imposition of a peculiarly American value that is not shared by all Western democracies). In mid-1990, Iliescu bowed to this pressure and agreed to permit a private television station. The U.S. government assigned

85

the International Media Fund the task of helping to get the station going.

In this case, the U.S. assistance role was not that of giving a boost to a functioning organization (as it had been with *România Liberă*), but rather of helping an organization get going essentially from scratch. To this end, the International Media Fund involved itself in many ways with the small group of Romanians who constituted the initial force behind the venture—developing a guiding plan for the station, choosing a board of directors, paying for all the studio equipment, training the staff, negotiating with government officials for permits and regulations, and providing wide-ranging technical support. Despite this multi-faceted, relatively high-cost effort, the television station, known as SOTI, was a failure.

SOTI did become operational in late 1991 and broadcasted programs for about a year. Its programs were of low quality, both technically and substantively, and SOTI failed to gain a stable, substantial market share. SOTI's financial situation was poor despite the U.S. assistance, and the station showed no sign of long-term viability. SOTI was openly pro-opposition and thus, like *România Liberă*, represented the growth of independent media only in the limited, anti-government sense of the term. The station's directors fought with each other constantly and demonstrated little understanding of the television business. Beset with technical, financial, and personnel problems, SOTI stopped broadcasting in 1993.

Why did SOTI fail? The Romanian government certainly did not make its task easy; at every step of the way, it put up obstacles. Despite Iliescu's formal permission for the station, obtaining a broadcasting license proved slow and difficult. The Romanian authorities ended up issuing a license for broadcasting only in the Bucharest area, not nationally. SOTI was allowed to broadcast only a few hours in the morning and in the evening. These obstacles and various others that arose were significant, but SOTI's demise was mostly rooted in its own internal problems. Two explanations for SOTI's failure are typically advanced by persons in Romania who followed SOTI closely. One is that SOTI's board and staff simply were not up to the job. The board members proved inept at business, unable to work together, and uninterested in really making the station succeed. The staff was technically weak and generally inexperienced. A second explanation—one that is widely held in Bucharest among people who followed SOTI's fortunes—is that SOTI was sabotaged by one or two key board members who were government "plants" who joined the board with the express purpose of destroying the organization.

Whichever explanation is correct (and they may both be true), two lessons stand out. First, it is extraordinarily difficult for an external donor agency to help develop from scratch an organization in another country if that type of organization has never before existed in that country and if local impetus for its development is weak. SOTI was not quite—but almost—an example of foreign implantation. A small local effort to get a private television station going did exist in 1990, but the foreign interest in the venture was much greater and ended up outweighing the local interest. In such circumstances, it is essential to nurture the local commitment to the project to ensure that foreign assistance does not get ahead of the local commitment itself. This approach was not taken in the SOTI case.

Second, if an external agency decides to go ahead and help establish a major new venture in a setting where only weak local commitment exists, then it must set aside its concern about micro-managing and accept that it will *have* to get involved on a day-to-day, hands-on basis for the first several years of the new organization's life. Though its assistance role was extensive and multi-faceted, the International Media Fund simply did not get involved in the SOTI project on a day-to-day basis. Media Fund representatives say they did not want to play too intensive a role in SOTI's operations. This is an understandable sentiment, and one appropriate for more conventional assistance projects. But for a project such as SOTI, it is a recipe for failure.

CHAPTER 4

IMPACT AND OTHER INQUIRIES

THE QUESTION OF EFFECTS

MODEST POSITIVE RESULTS

The positive effects of U.S. democracy assistance programs in Romania have ranged from modest to negligible, with most programs producing at least some positive effects, no programs producing decisive results, and a few outright failures. The assistance to the Romanian opposition parties has produced only minor improvements with respect to the many basic weaknesses of those parties. The elections assistance—both the technical assistance to the Romanian electoral authorities and the international and domestic monitoring efforts—helped improve somewhat the administration of the 1992 local and national elections. The rule-of-law programs have exposed members of the Romanian legal community to Western legal ideas and models but have not significantly altered the troubled Romanian judicial system or strengthened the rule of law. Parliamentary assistance has produced a few changes in the Parliament's rules and methods of operation and perhaps some attitudinal changes among individual parliamentarians, but it has not resulted in any noticeable amelioration of the basically problematic nature of that institution.

The U.S. assistance to civic advocacy organizations has contributed to the development of a growing new sector of non-governmental organizations; in some areas, such as the environment and human rights, civic advocacy organizations have had some positive effects on governmental policy, and they have begun to raise public understanding, at least in major cities, with respect to some social and political issues. The aid to Romanian unions has introduced some Romanian unionists to U.S. ideas about union-building and strengthened in a modest fashion two union confederations—one that ended up moving closer to the government and one that is relatively independent of the government. U.S. media assistance has strengthened the position of the most widely circulated pro-opposition newspaper and helped keep afloat a number of small

89

intellectual publications of a generally pro-opposition character. It did not succeed in helping establish a viable private television station in Bucharest. The assistance for local government has helped increase the technical capacities of mayors' offices in three cities. The educational assistance and visitor programs have exposed a number of Romanians to different aspects of U.S. society and enabled some Romanians to gain Western training in different fields relevant to democratic institution-building.

A corollary to this general conclusion of a very modest level of effects is that, to the extent that U.S. assistance has had discernible effects on Romanian organizations, it has been less to shape them in accordance with U.S.-conceived pro-democratic blueprints than to strengthen their own basic nature. Whether newly formed or deeply entrenched, those Romanian organizations that have benefited from U.S. assistance have in many cases proven to be very much their own bosses, with their own methods and goals. Sometimes these methods and goals conform to those of their foreign backers, but often they do not. The U.S. experiences with the Democratic Convention, *Frăţia*, *România Liberă*, and the Parliament, for example, all highlight the basic corollary. This finding goes against the frequent assumption of U.S. and other foreign assistance providers that by providing assistance they exert significant influence over what often appear to be weak, malleable institutions.

The conclusion that the U.S. democracy assistance has had only modest effects does not of course mean that the United States (and other Western democracies) on the whole have had only very limited effect on Romania's political development since 1989. Obviously, Western influence on Romania and other Eastern European countries exists at many levels, including the commercial, cultural, diplomatic, political, and others. The attractive model of Western democracy and capitalism is a driving force behind the whole project of post-communist transition in Romania and other countries of the region. And since 1989, Romania's leaders have shaped their domestic political agendas and undertakings with an almost constant eye on how the West will perceive and judge their actions. Romanian leaders want the approval of Western governments, both for psychological reasons relating to the ardent desire of many Romanians for their country to be accepted as a full-fledged member of "the West," and for the tangible security and economic benefits that good relations with the United States and

Western Europe can bring. These leaders are well aware that obtaining such approval requires at least a certain degree of conformance to Western democratic norms. This general influence on the political evolution of Romania and other countries of the region is profound, but it is not controlling, as evidenced by the only very partial democratization achieved in a number of countries including not only Romania but also Slovakia, Albania, and Bulgaria.

Returning to the U.S. assistance programs, one can ask why they have had only modest or even negligible positive effects. One explanation stands out: the overall magnitude of the assistance has been extremely small relative to the task. The total of U.S. government funds spent on promoting democracy in Romania in the first five years after the fall of Ceauşescu was approximately $13.5 million, or about 60 cents per Romanian over those five years. Most of this assistance reached Romanians only indirectly in the form of training and technical assistance delivered by U.S. intermediary organizations.

It must be understood that the U.S. democracy assistance effort in Romania, and indeed in the former communist countries of Central and Eastern Europe generally since 1989, has consisted of little more than tinkering around the edges of the complex challenges that these societies face. Summing up the effort as mere "tinkering" may seem harsh. This conclusion is not, however, intended to imply a lack of commitment on the part of the many dedicated individuals in the U.S. government and the intermediary organizations that have carried out the assistance. Rather, it is a characterization of the overall magnitude of the effort. How else to describe a judicial reform effort that attempts, with $100,000 per year, to make a dent in a profoundly troubled judicial system that has no modern history of independence or competence? How else to describe a parliamentary assistance program that aims to improve the functioning of a deeply stagnant, polarized political institution with a few series of seminars? The same question could be asked about every area of the democracy assistance programming. The effects of the democracy assistance may be modest, but they have been generally commensurate with the outlay.

When one steps back and considers the enormity of the task of democratization in a country such as Romania—drastically altering the basic relationship of the individual to the state, reshaping the very notion and limits of what is political, and transforming a fundamentally undemocratic state apparatus—the democracy

91

assistance programs appear as dots on a large screen. The U.S. assistance effort in Romania and other countries in the region is not a 1950s-style Marshall Plan embrace; it is a 1990s pat on the back.

The ongoing debate in Washington about the value of democracy assistance and other forms of aid to the region seems divorced from this reality. Skeptics demand to see proof that small doses of democracy assistance are bringing democracy to countries with politically calamitous pasts. Proponents ascribe extraordinary links of causation between aid programs and political progress in countries that do manage to move ahead. It might be better if democracy assistance programs were not characterized as such, but merely as programs to promote greater pluralism or representation or participation. The term "democracy promotion" too easily overexcites the American mind; once we label a set of activities, no matter how minor, as "democracy promotion," we expect it to achieve that enormous goal.

An additional explanation for the modest effects of democracy assistance in Romania is that in many cases the assistance has been directed to institutions in which there is little impetus toward reform. If a justice ministry has little real interest in reforming the judicial system, or the dominant parties in a parliament fear that institutional change may favor opposition forces or lead to the loss of perquisites, then small training programs, transfers of equipment, and visitor exchanges with those institutions are unlikely to have much positive effect. In general, post-1989 U.S. democracy assistance in Romania, and in Central and Eastern Europe generally, is most effective when it seeks to help people and organizations that already are trying to move in a democratic direction (broadly defined) to do so with greater certainty, speed, and depth. It cannot for the most part substitute for or create a will to reform that does not already exist. Since in Romania many sectors of political society both within and outside the power structure have not demonstrated any strong, self-generated impetus toward reform, the U.S. assistance, as well as the assistance from other Western countries, has encountered many frustrations.

The assistance programs that most clearly have had positive effects are those which have supported people or organizations already committed to carrying out pro-democratic activities. U.S. (and European) assistance clearly has been useful, for example, for stimulating the growth of the NGO sector in Romania, and the NGO sector is one of the most significant positive developments in the socio-political arena since 1990. Some distinctive features of the NGO assistance have helped make it successful. These include the willingness of some donors to transfer funds directly to Romanian organizations instead of channeling the funds primarily through U.S. intermediary organizations, as well as the small size of the recipient organizations, which has made it easier to get the assistance to the best people. But at root, assistance in this sector has been particularly productive because a number of dynamic, motivated people in the Romanian NGO world are engaged in building organizations and carrying out activities—people who are ready and willing to make good use of external assistance.

A further explanation of the generally modest effects of U.S. democracy assistance relates to its design. As discussed in more detail below in the section on implementation, the technical assistance provided by U.S. organizations has not always been well designed, and the bulk of funds often have ended up going to U.S. organizations rather than to local actors. And whether well designed or not, the sort of technical assistance that has made up most U.S. democracy assistance in the region—primarily short-term training—by its very nature has only slowly emerging and almost inevitably minor effects. Many types of people have been trained through U.S. programs—notably parliamentarians, judges, journalists, party activists, union leaders, election administrators, election observers, human rights advocates, and teachers. Trying to change people's behavior by modifying their knowledge and attitudes without changing the external incentives, constraints, and institutional contexts in which they must operate is very difficult. Training is not useless as a form of democracy assistance, but it is a much more limited tool than many of its proponents seem to understand. Unrealistic expectations of training programs are fueled by the apparent belief of at least some of the persons working in the U.S. assistance organizations that Western liberal democracy is essentially a natural political form that will, once explained, dissolve countervailing historical patterns and embedded structural obstacles. In this view, once Romanians are exposed to the basic principles of how a parliament works, what judicial independence is, how to campaign for office, or how to write non-partisan news stories, they will have a "now I get it!" epiphany and act differently forever after.

THE NEGATIVE SIDE OF THE LEDGER

When discussing the vexing question of how to assess the effects of their work, those involved in U.S. democracy assistance often acknowledge the difficulty of that inquiry but then add with a shrug, "at least we're not doing any harm." In fact, however, unanticipated negative effects do sometimes result from democracy assistance programs. Two types of negative consequences of U.S. democracy assistance can be identified in Romania. Like the positive effects of the assistance, they are modest in magnitude but still worth noting. First, because a sizable portion of them has clearly favored the Romanian opposition, the U.S. assistance programs have aggravated a siege mentality among some persons within the power structure about relations with the United States and the West generally. In the words of one former Romanian official who had been told by a U.S. assistance organization that he could not attend one of its training seminars because that organization considered his party non-democratic, "If you treat us like bastards, we'll be bastards." The general implications of such a partisan approach to assistance are explored more fully in the section below on strategy.

Second, like any form of foreign assistance, democracy assistance runs the risk of creating harmful dependency relationships, in which obtaining assistance becomes an end in itself rather than a means to an end for people and organizations in the recipient countries. Assistance recipients can come to believe that external assistance, rather than their own effort, can solve their country's problems. Such attitudes over the long term result in both bitterness on the part of the aid recipients when the assistance eventually falls short of their unrealistic expectations, and in paralysis when the assistance paradoxically ends up weakening rather strengthening their own self-motivation.

As mentioned in Chapter 3, there are signs of this phenomenon in the assistance relationship between the Romanian opposition parties and IRI (and other Western backers of the opposition parties). But other areas of democracy assistance manifest it as well. Many of the recipients of U.S. democracy assistance show at least traces of a dependency mindset. In Romanian NGO, media, and union circles, for example, I encountered people caught between wanting assistance and resenting it in equal measure. I also met people who were so tantalized by the prospect of obtaining Western funding that they had come to see it as a goal in itself. In one provincial city, a young man who had recently attended a U.S.-sponsored seminar on NGO development told me his career goal was now to be head of a Western-funded NGO. When I asked what he wanted to achieve through such work, his answer was vague. All that was clear to him was that NGO work was where the foreign money was flowing and where Westerners thought talented young Romanians should be.

THE ALL-IMPORTANT SUBJECTIVE SIDE

The above assessment of the effects of U.S. democracy assistance concentrates on the same external, institution-oriented level of effects in terms of which the programs are explicitly designed. Yet in talking with Romanians about their perceptions of the effects of U.S. and other foreign-sponsored democracy assistance programs, I found that they often spoke in very different terms. They highlighted the psychological, moral, and emotional effects of assistance—a set of effects at the personal more than the institutional level that I will here call, for lack of a better term, the subjective effects of assistance.

Some of these subjective effects occur at the very general level of moral support. Many of the Romanians I interviewed who have been involved with U.S. democracy assistance programs told me that the assistance has provided them with moral and emotional support that has been more important than the particular strengths and weaknesses of specific programs. Many in the political opposition—feeling that they have been fighting a lonely, uphill struggle against an entrenched, almost omnipotent power structure—have viewed U.S. assistance as a welcome sign of support, particularly in the initial period after the fall of Ceauşescu. Such moral support has reached beyond the opposition community as well. Whatever their political outlook or their degree of interest in politics, many Romanians have a powerful, long pent-up desire for contact with the West and for having their lives and their country essentially be joined to the West. The U.S. democracy assistance programs have represented a hand extended by the United States to Romania— a recognition by the United States that, politically, Romania can and should be a "normal Western country," as Romanians like to say. For reasons discussed below in the section on conflicting perceptions, the moral support conveyed early on by U.S. assistance has to some extent been replaced in recent years by a sense of let-down and even bitterness among Romanians, especially in the opposition parties. But even those who are now disappointed by what they see as an inadequate amount of assistance say the early sense of support was very helpful to them.

Other subjective effects occur at a more specific level, which, at the risk of using an overused term, involves the capacity of assistance to help "empower" individuals. Communism in Romania had many devastating effects, but its most profound, pervasive legacy was the crushing dis-empowerment of individuals—the creation of near-complete dependence on a centralized state as a way of life. In describing the effects of U.S. and other foreign-sponsored democracy assistance programs, participants frequently report that the assistance helped them begin to assert themselves, to channel their talents and energies toward definable goals. Such learning processes involve a series of elements that often do not unfold in any identifiable order but that eventually add up to a coherent whole: how to believe in the possibility of change, how to conceptualize and define goals, how to relate individual actions to larger goals, how to articulate interests and goals publicly, and how to mobilize people to work together toward a goal.

These things are in fact rarely taught specifically in the assistance programs but rather are learned by doing and by working collaboratively with Americans or persons from other democratic societies. What Romanians have needed to learn, as they frequently say, is something extraordinarily basic but sweeping: "how an individual behaves in a democracy."[35]

Romanians talk at length about these subjective effects when asked about the impact of democracy assistance. Moreover, when asked to compare the significance of such effects to more formalized institutional effects of assistance, they usually say the subjective effects are much more important. It is those effects, they say, that will last, that can be applied in other situations, and that can be passed along by them to others—because those are the effects that represent deep-seated changes in individual character rather than just new arrangements or rearrangements of institutional forms and processes.

It is perhaps not surprising that Romanians emphasize the greater importance of the subjective over the objective effects of assistance in those areas of assistance where the objective effects have been clearly weak. Interestingly, however, this view is just as prevalent among those Romanians who have participated in projects that have clearly produced positive objective effects. Many people working with the Romanian civic advocacy NGOs, for example, take pride in the accomplishments of their organizations and credit external assistance as having been crucial to those accomplishments. Nonetheless, they almost uniformly respond to questions about the effects of assistance by saying that the positive changes in themselves and their colleagues as people, as socio-political actors, are much more important than the particular activities of their organizations.

It is very difficult to assess the subjective effects of democracy assistance in any quantifiable fashion. They are psychological, emotional, moral—elusively amorphous and qualitative. In addition, they involve long-term chains of action and result, learning and consequent behavior, that are impossible to pin down in any simple way. This is evident from the many stories of people who have participated in assistance programs—how one initial positive experience may lead to some later challenge that ends up resulting in further achievements. Tracing the paths of Romanians, especially young Romanians, who have been part of democracy assistance programs, I saw numerous cases of remarkable personal development—from member of a student group to head of a large civic organization, from assistant in a small political party program to local director of a major administrative reform program, and from conventional lawyer to director of a human rights organization. Such cases are not examples of mere career advancement; they are highly telescoped transformations of talented but inexperienced persons into significant socio-political actors.

Yet because the subjective effects of assistance are what they are, namely subjective, they do not fit into the increasingly quantitative, reductionistic grids that the U.S. government insists on using to evaluate democracy assistance. They are not, in the bureaucratic terms that now dominate the assistance field, "measurable deliverables." The Romanians who have participated extensively with U.S. assistance programs are well aware of this gap between what they believe is actually most significant about the assistance and what the assistance providers look for in their "objective" evaluations. These Romanians are puzzled that the United States comes to their society, expends extensive amounts of time and energy promoting democracy, but then imposes a narrow *post-hoc* framework of evaluation that produces only a formalistic, inadequate understanding of what the assistance has actually achieved.

STRATEGY
THE CHECKLIST APPROACH

As they scrambled to respond to the dramatic, unanticipated political events of 1989 in Central and Eastern Europe, U.S.

97

assistance providers had little time to spend formulating strategies of democracy promotion. Driven by the fear that if the United States did not rush in with support for the democratic transitions, the whole wave of political change might stall or even be reversed, they were concerned primarily with getting assistance under way as quickly as possible. One high-level official responsible for U.S. assistance to the region told me that throughout 1990 she had a recurrent nightmare in which U.S. assistance did not get going quickly, communism returned to the region, and she was singled out for blame.

In this situation of maximal hurry and minimal reflection, U.S. assistance providers adopted a common-sense strategy of democracy assistance that can be called "the checklist approach." This approach can be summarized as a three-part syllogism. First, democracy is defined in terms of a checklist made up of the major institutional features of U.S. democracy: free and fair elections, ideologically moderate national political parties, an independent judiciary, a strong national legislature, active local government, independent trade unions, a large number of private television and radio stations, newspapers and magazines, and a wide array of policy-oriented NGOs. Second, democratization is assumed to be the process of establishing those institutions or transforming the existing local ones to resemble the U.S. versions. Third, democracy assistance is to be directed to help accomplish the establishment or transformation of local institutions to correspond to the checklist.

In Romania, the U.S. government has pursued a particular variation of the checklist approach—a partisan strategy. Before discussing that strategy, it is worth highlighting several problems with the general checklist approach that the United States has employed throughout the region since 1989. One problem concerns the underlying model of democracy. U.S. assistance practitioners often try to present the democracy checklist as a generic list that corresponds not to a particular American definition of democracy but to a much broader concept of Western liberal democracy. In fact, however, the checklist does reflect very particular American ways of thinking about democracy, as discussed in the previous chapter on specific areas of assistance. These American ideas about the desired forms of democracy may not always be of interest to or appropriate for other societies. Recalling examples cited earlier, in the U.S. view, national legislatures are supposed to be independent, powerful institutions that serve as a counterweight to executive branch power; this conception, however, cannot just be transplanted to the parliamentary and mixed presidential-parliamentary systems of Central and Eastern Europe. Similarly, the adversarial U.S. model of union organization and labor relations may not be suitable in countries oriented to the continental tradition of tripartite business-labor-government structures. And the U.S. emphasis on policy-oriented NGOs as a major part of a democratic system is not shared by many European societies.

A second problem with the checklist approach is that it encourages assistance providers to not set priorities but just try a little bit of everything. The checklist is very long and is usually formulated as a non-hierarchical assemblage of objectives, all of which are considered crucial. In many Central and Eastern European countries, USAID funds a separate project for each item on the checklist, usually with different U.S. intermediary organizations responsible for individual projects. Each project is carried out relatively independently of the others, the idea being that because the different projects are drawn from the overarching checklist, they are working toward a single, coherent endpoint. Criteria for weighting assistance toward particular items on the checklist are usually absent. The result is that the available assistance is spread among a long list of program areas, with no single area getting enough support to have a major impact.

Third, conceiving of democratization as primarily a set of institutional endpoints leads assistance practitioners to pay insufficient attention to the actual constituent processes of democratization. Defining the key institutional features of an established democratic system reveals little about how a partially democratic or largely undemocratic society can achieve them. The model of process assumed in the checklist approach—the notion that people must be shown how to conduct or rebuild their institutions in the image of correspondent institutions in established democracies—is superficial and mechanistic. Missing from this model is the fact that the institutional features of an established democracy represent the outcomes of long-term experience with balancing power and interests between competing sectors in a society. Such balances, compromises, and accords formalize the underlying socio-political consensus of a democracy. It is not possible to achieve them by merely replicating a certain institutional architecture.

THE PARTISAN APPROACH

The United States basically has pursued the checklist approach to democratic development in all of the countries of the region.

In some countries, however, it has emphasized a particular variation of the approach—a partisan strategy in which democracy
assistance is used to help strengthen one side of the political spectrum relative to the other. The partisan strategy is rooted in an anti-
communist perspective and employed accordingly. In countries
such as Poland, Hungary, and Czechoslovakia, where U.S. policy-
makers and assistance providers perceived in 1989 and 1990 that
the political transitions had involved a genuine shattering of the
communist power structure, the United States has taken a consciously multi-partisan approach. In other countries, however, such
as Romania, Bulgaria, and Albania, where the U.S. perception was
that the communist power structures were still substantially in place
after the political events of 1989, the United States has pursued the
partisan strategy. The thrust of this approach is that U.S. democracy
assistance (and U.S. policy generally) should strengthen those political forces which seek to challenge and if possible defeat the former
communist forces.

In Romania, the partisan approach has been a major feature
of the U.S. democracy assistance effort, especially in the 1990-92
period. IRI has been the lead partisan actor, attempting to help the
opposition political parties defeat the government and excluding
the governing parties from its party assistance. Many other assistance programs, including the support for *Frăţia*, *România Liberă*,
SOTI, the Group for Social Dialogue, and the Romanian Students
League, have been rooted in the notion that promoting democracy
means helping a certain part of the political spectrum, i.e., the
opposition, gain power. Moreover, the overall thrust of the U.S.
diplomatic line in the 1990-92 period supported the partisan assistance approach, with many U.S. officials making very clear their
sympathy for the opposition and their hope for its success in the
1992 elections.

It was probably inevitable that most of the U.S. organizations
involved in promoting democracy in Romania (and other southern-
tier countries) after 1989 would gravitate toward the partisan
approach. In countries where struggling new anti-communist forces
were competing against revamped former communists still holding
many of the cards, many Americans arriving in the region quickly
concluded that these societies could be neatly divided between
anti-communists and former communists and that the United States
must help the former defeat the latter. Understandable though it
may have been, the partisan approach nonetheless has, at least in

Romania, proved to be problematic in significant ways. This is a fact that U.S. policymakers should bear in mind as they consider assistance strategies in other transitional countries, such as Russia, where the United States feels drawn toward a partisan role out of a similar desire to help steer the society toward a reformist path by taking sides between contending political groups.

One important problem with the partisan approach is that democracy assistance is ill-suited to serving as a political battering ram. At best democracy assistance can produce gradual, incremental changes in institutions or political balances, changes which do not correspond to the pressure for rapid, decisive results that typically drives partisan engagements. U.S. democracy assistance is very rarely of such a magnitude as to be able to have major effects on entrenched power structures. Setting such a task for assistance ensures that disappointment will result and that whatever minor positive effects are actually achieved will appear inadequate.

A second problem is that a partisan approach creates unproductive hostilities on the part of those against whom the assistance is targeted. As discussed in the analysis of IRI's political party assistance, partisan assistance by large external actors contributes to a siege mentality among persons within the power structure, strengthening their resistance to change instead of fostering change. It is striking what a strong negative association many Romanian officials have with the mere idea of U.S.-sponsored efforts to promote democracy in their country. Due to the partisan nature of much of the early U.S. democracy assistance, Romanian officials instinctively equate "promoting democracy" with efforts to oust them from power, and are therefore reflexively negative toward all democracy assistance.

This general negative association results in what was described in the analysis of political party assistance as a "coloring effect"—a partisan approach in some parts of an assistance portfolio inevitably colors other parts of the portfolio. As noted earlier, most Romanians have little understanding of the differences between the various U.S. organizations involved in democracy assistance programs in Romania. They tend to lump them all together as "the Americans" and to assume that the activities of all of the organizations (with the particular exception of the Soros Foundations, which are identified so closely with the singular figure of George Soros) are direct expressions of U.S. policy. Consequently, the fact that some parts of the U.S. democracy assistance are openly pro-opposition encourages or permits Romanian officials to view all parts of the assistance that way. This wholesale reaction has hurt U.S. efforts to promote the concept of civil society development as a nonpartisan cause that all Romanians should support; it feeds the suspicions of Romanian officials that U.S. assistance for Romanian NGOs such as human rights groups and civic education groups is serving a pro-opposition agenda. The coloring effect even spreads beyond the democracy-assistance sphere. When the Romanian-American Enterprise Fund was established in 1995, some Romanian officials, conditioned to think of U.S. aid as being pro-opposition, initially took a skeptical view of the Fund, assuming that it would in some way be used against the government.

A third problem with the partisan approach is that it fosters divisions within the recipient country. Partisan assistance involves U.S. organizations with only superficial knowledge of the recipient society, drawing sharp political lines between people and between organizations in that society, categorizing some as good and others as bad, including some and excluding others. Such line-drawing often angers and alienates people in the recipient country. Its inherent divisiveness can also work against any process of democratization based on increased cooperation, reconciliation, and interconnections among people and institutions. Interestingly, I encountered strong objections to the U.S. partisan approach as much from Romanian civic activists, few of whom are at all sympathetic to the government, as from Romanian officials. The activists object vigorously to the tendency of some U.S. assistance organizations to come to Romania and affix the label of "democrat" to some people and "non-democrat" to others. Such an approach, they say, is not only often empirically wrong; it also fuels the unproductive, "no compromise" moralistic political outlook of some leaders of the Romanian opposition parties. This political outlook aggravates many people in Romania's emerging civil society who are generally not sympathetic to the government, but who are highly frustrated with the opposition parties.

The partisan approach must be questioned not only because the positive effects it has produced have been small and probably less significant than the various negative side effects it has engendered, but also because the political evolution of Romania since 1990 has greatly weakened the original basis of the approach. Whatever plausibility the black-and-white view of Romanian politics had in 1990 has significantly faded in the intervening years as Romanian politics have come to be a canvas painted in many shades of gray. The political forces governing Romania are scarcely shining democrats, but they have nonetheless overseen a process of at least partial democratization in which Romania has become a much more open, pluralistic society than it was in 1990. And the opposition forces no longer fit very neatly under the early, appealing label of "struggling democratic forces." The opposition has proven to contain quite heterogeneous political tendencies, including monarchists and fairly intolerant nationalists, and has neither exerted great energy to better its own situation nor exhibited much obvious capacity to actually run a country. The idea that democratization in Romania will only really occur if the opposition wins national elections and takes power, a central tenet of the black-and-white view, is no longer persuasive and finds few proponents in Romania outside the narrowest of opposition party circles. Other socio-political factors, such as the growth of the private business sector and the rise of civil society generally, seem much more important to Romania's democratization than the particular fortunes of the opposition parties.

A final issue with respect to the partisan approach is a very general one concerning sovereignty and political intervention: Is it right for the United States, or any other powerful foreign country, to intervene in another country's electoral processes with the express purpose of helping one side against the other? The answer might seem an absolute "no," but the issue is open to some debate. The International Republican Institute, which is the main (though not the only) publicly funded U.S. organization that openly carries out such partisan interventions, bases its actions on the rationale of helping "to level the playing field" in foreign elections. Elections in many transitional countries, IRI representatives argue, are plagued by serious inequalities between entrenched political forces of dubious democratic intent and struggling pro-democratic opposition forces. If the United States wishes to support free and fair elections, they contend, how can it simply stand aside and let such distortions dictate the results? Assistance by external actors to the disadvantaged side is necessary to allow at least a chance of a fair election.

A plausible case for such an approach can be made in some situations of first-time elections in which a dictatorial regime, bowing to domestic or international pressure, is holding elections and a nascent opposition is scrambling to compete despite many serious handicaps. The Chilean plebiscite of 1988 and the extensive U.S.

and Western European assistance to the local political forces opposing General Pinochet is one example of such a case. But in a country, such as Romania, that has gone through at least one cycle of national elections judged by the international community to have been at least reasonably free and fair, and that continues to have a relatively open, pluralistic political life, partisan interventions are of questionable legitimacy.

It is true that in such situations—as IRI representatives stress is the case with Romania—the ruling party maintains significant advantages in terms of finances, access to the media, and the ability to use economic levers for political ends. But such inequalities are not sufficient to justify foreign partisan interventions. In many countries that the United States recognizes as democratic, ruling parties hold or have held huge advantages over opposition parties. For example, the advantages in terms of finances, media access, and economic levers held for decades by the Liberal Democratic Party of Japan over its rivals were very much on the order of those held by the PDSR in Romania. This is not to say that such inequalities are healthy in democratic terms, only that they are not in and of themselves grounds for U.S. partisan intervention in another country's electoral processes.

ALTERNATIVE APPROACHES

Since President Iliescu's victory in the 1992 elections, the partisan approach has faded somewhat in U.S. democracy assistance programs in Romania. As discussed in Chapter 2, U.S. assistance programs are now in a mixed state. Some are still partisan, either in design (like IRI's continuing assistance to the opposition parties) or in spirit (like those of FTUI and IDEE, which are still operating from a black-and-white view of Romanian politics). Others follow a loosely defined nonpartisan approach, which embodies one or both of two theories about how a deepening of democratization will occur in Romania. Neither of these theories is very clearly articulated by the assistance providers, but both are plausible, and each is a better basis for assistance than the partisan approach.

One of the two theories is that the motor of further democratization in Romania will be a continuation of the gradual process of change in socio-political values that is occurring among Romanians as they have more direct and indirect contact with the West and more experience at home with political pluralism and open-ness. U.S. and other foreign-sponsored democracy assistance pro-grams can support this process of values change, assistance provid-ers believe, by providing Romanians opportunities to go to the West, bringing Western information into Romania, and supporting local efforts to foster pluralism, openness, and other democratic values among Romanians. Civic education programs, media assis-tance, NGO support, and educational programs are examples of activities that reflect this idea. The main limitation of this approach (or, more precisely, the main characteristic of this approach, which U.S. assistance providers tend to consider a limitation) is its slow, gradualistic nature. Encouraging a process of values change prom-ises little immediate impact and no dramatic results.

The other theory increasingly operative in U.S. democracy assistance is that the key problem with Romania's political life is the continued centralization of power. In this view, democracy assistance should focus on strengthening centers of power in Roma-nian society outside the control or strong influence of the central state and government. Thus, assistance should help bolster sectors such as the media, unions, the business sector, local government, and the NGO sector. This approach resembles the partisan approach to some extent in that it helps those who seek to challenge the power structure, but it differs from an openly pro-opposition, anti-government approach in several important ways.

One key difference is that a "decentralization of power" approach does not focus on elections as the key mechanism of long-term democratic development. It does not aim to try to pro-duce certain results in the elections or, more generally, concentrate assistance on the electoral process. Another difference is that under such an approach, assistance providers encourage non-state actors to work with the government when it is possible to do so in a productive, non-dependent way rather than urge a reflexively hands-off, confrontational relationship with the government. This approach is also friendly to assistance programs that try to include people from the power structure when possible—to help "social-ize" such people in the language and activities of democracy assis-tance rather than shut them out altogether.

The "decentralization of power" approach is reflected in some of the new U.S. democracy assistance programs that have been developed since the 1992 elections, such as the Civic Voice pro-gram, the Democracy Network program, and the local government program. It is still sometimes confused with the partisan approach, on both the U.S. and the Romanian sides, because of the legacy of partisanship in the U.S. assistance and the failure of the U.S. government to conceive of and articulate the strategy as a clear replacement of the earlier approach. The main uncertainty about this approach is whether the modest amounts of assistance involved are enough to significantly strengthen centers of power outside what remains a highly dominant centralized state.

THE SEPARATE WORLDS OF ECONOMIC AND POLITICAL ASSISTANCE

The U.S. democracy assistance programs in Romania exist alongside much larger programs of U.S. economic assistance. This study focuses only on the political side of the assistance picture. Nonetheless a few points about the relationship between the economic and political sides are relevant to the broader question of strategy. As we have seen, U.S. policy toward Central and Eastern Europe since 1989 has been based on the idea that transitions to democracy and market economies are mutually reinforcing. By increasing the free flow of information, empowering individuals, and making governments more accountable, U.S. officials argue, democratization will facilitate the transition to a market economy. In parallel fashion, by establishing private property, reducing the leverage of the state over the lives of individuals, and raising the overall socio-economic level of the population, the transition to a market economy can strengthen democratization. The many complexities and even points of contradiction in simultaneous transitions to democracy and market economics—a subject that has received increasing attention among academics and policy analysts in recent years—do not figure significantly in the U.S. policy formulation.[36]

U.S. officials consider U.S. economic and political assistance programs in Central and Eastern Europe to be complementary. In practice, however, these programs are pursued as largely separate domains. The U.S. economic assistance to Romania is not designed or implemented on the basis of any significant analysis of the political effects of the assistance—other than the very general (and not very closely thought out) notion that economic programs which reduce the state's role in the economy will tend to reduce the state's means of exerting political control over citizens. This lack of consideration of the political effects of economic assistance is true even in the case of projects that obviously have important political ramifications, such as assistance for the privatization of agricultural land.

Similarly, most U.S. democracy assistance is not designed or implemented with much consideration of its possible economic effects. Again, this is true even for projects with evident potential for crossover effects, such as the assistance to strengthen Romania's labor unions. The economic and political components of U.S. assistance in Romania (and in the rest of the region) are described in separate sections of USAID reports, strategy statements, and other documents. They involve largely non-overlapping sets of U.S. intermediary organizations and non-overlapping worlds of Romanian participants.

In the past several years, however, some nascent connections between U.S. economic and political assistance in Romania have been emerging. With the heightened focus on civil society development in U.S. democracy assistance, a progressively wider circle of Romanian NGOs is being included in projects aimed at building democracy by strengthening NGOs. These local NGOs no longer always have only politics-related themes such as human rights and civic education as their main area of work; they now sometimes focus on more economics-related concerns such as public health, agriculture, and the environment. In short, assistance programs involving NGOs increasingly relate explicitly to both democracy promotion and economic reform. Such projects are also starting to be tied to local government issues, further intermixing economic and political concerns.[37] These economic-political connections in U.S. assistance to Romania are very tentative and exploratory, however, and do not substantially change the basic separation of the two domains.

IMPLEMENTATION

THE NON-DEVELOPMENTAL APPROACH

The implementation of U.S. government-sponsored democracy assistance in Romania, which has largely been carried out by U.S. intermediary organizations, has suffered from a number of serious problems. The most obvious of these—a problem to which critics of all types of U.S. assistance in Eastern Europe and the former Soviet Union frequently point—is that the vast majority of assistance dollars have ended up going to U.S. organizations rather than to people or organizations within the recipient countries.[38]

This problem is really the result of donor-agency inability to correct a series of more specific shortcomings in the basic methods of assistance implementation.

One shortcoming has been the failure of most U.S. intermediary organizations to build up any significant local staff in Romania. Most of these organizations, even ones that have now been operating in Romania for over five years, still depend upon one or two American representatives working almost alone in Bucharest—the local staff being limited to a translator or two and occasionally an office administrator—to design and oversee the implementation of their activities. One instructive exception to this pattern has been the work of IFES on civil society development. As IFES carried out its Civic Voice project from 1993 to 1995, its U.S. local representative built up a talented, dynamic local staff. This staff became deeply involved in all aspects of the project, functioning not just as minor administrative assistants but as the people designing and implementing the program. When the project drew to a close in 1995, the local staff decided to stay together as a self-standing Romanian civic education organization.

Compared to using a lone U.S. representative, building up a local staff has many advantages beyond the financial savings involved (local personnel usually cost far less, often by a factor of 10 or 20, than U.S. personnel based in the country). A local staff can give the U.S. organization much greater capacity to understand the actors, political dynamics, and underlying realities of the local situation. It also contributes a partial local coloring, lowering sensitivities about foreign intervention and encouraging participants in the assistance to take responsibility for the projects. Furthermore, such an approach brings the added benefit of giving sustained training to local persons in the substantive areas of the assistance as well as in the important areas of finance and management.

The extensive use by U.S. intermediary organizations of American local representatives was probably inevitable in the initial period after 1989, when the U.S. organizations were new to the country. But it is an approach that has worn very thin over the years. The local representatives are usually young—mid-twenties to early thirties—with little or no experience working abroad, little or no background in Eastern European affairs, and no Romanian language skills. They usually stay about one year, although a few have remained longer. Romanians do cite some positive features of the U.S. local representatives. Most have been hard-working and strongly committed to their projects. Many have projected an idealism about their work that has impressed the Romanians with whom they have worked. Being young and having no experience in the region, they have been willing to try new approaches and have not, at least upon arrival, been widely afflicted with defeatism or pessimism.

On the other hand, Romanians also report significant problems with the local representatives. Their youth and inexperience have led them to make significant and sometimes seriously incorrect judgments about local political actors, to make bad decisions about tactics and strategy in their projects, to exhibit a confusing mix of naiveté and arrogance, and to operate from a blank historical slate. Romanians have become very dissatisfied with the U.S. local representative method of operation. "We are tired of educating your local representatives," one Romanian political activist told me. "They come knowing nothing about us. We spend much time educating them. When they finally know enough about Romania to be effective, it is time for them to go. A new one comes and we start all over again. We don't want to do that any more."

A second major problem with the implementation of U.S. democracy assistance has been the heavy reliance for training and technical assistance on short-term visits by foreign experts (usually American, sometimes Western or Eastern European, Latin American, or Asian). Such experts come from outside the country for two- or three-day conferences or seminars at which they present information about a selected topic, such as NGO advocacy, election administration, judicial administration, investigative reporting, or the functioning of parliaments. Romanians acknowledge that short-term visiting foreign experts had some utility in the early 1990s, when Romania was just opening up. But they are very tired of them now. They complain that such visitors rarely know much about Romania and usually present information that is only marginally relevant to the Romanian context. The experts rarely return to do any follow-up work. Their visits often bear an unfortunate resemblance to political tourism.

The weariness with short-term visiting foreign experts is part of a larger syndrome of what might be called "conference fatigue" in Romania. U.S. and European democracy assistance projects in Romania frequently involve conferences and seminars. Many Romanians told me that their initial interest in and even excitement about foreign-sponsored conferences and seminars has been replaced by a deep skepticism and weariness, unless the events are organized by Romanians for the purpose of creating interchange among Romanians. They believe that conferences and seminars are badly overused as vehicles for transmitting information, knowledge, or skills between foreigners and Romanians. Such events are dominated, they say, by one-way sessions in which foreigners lecture to Romanians and present information not tailored to Romanian realities. The same relatively small circle of Romanians tends to be invited over and over to these conferences. Romanians who participate in such events have the strong impression that U.S. and European assistance organizations rely so heavily on conferences and seminars not because they really believe they are useful, but because such events are relatively easy to carry out (compared to more sustained forms of assistance) and because such events play well back in Washington, Brussels, or London.

A third problem has been that U.S. intermediary organizations in many cases have paid little attention to the crucial issue of local ownership, or "buy-in," of their assistance efforts. In too many cases they have been content to get their technical assistance out the door as quickly as possible, making little effort to develop their activities as truly collaborative ventures in which local partners play an active role in the planning and implementation of the assistance. In related fashion, too little attention has been given to the very basic development-assistance concept of local capacity-building. Very little assistance has gone directly to Romanian organizations. Programs to train trainers, for example, have been surprisingly rare. Sustainability of the assistance undertakings is often an afterthought, assigned to the Romanian side without notice and late in the process. Furthermore, U.S. organizations have made little effort to identify and nurture local sources of expertise, such as universities, technical institutes, and businesses, often reflexively (and incorrectly) assuming that no one in the country knows anything useful about the technical areas at issue.

These various shortcomings in the implementation of democracy assistance are all part of what can be called the non-developmental approach of much of U.S. democracy assistance in Romania (and Central and Eastern Europe generally). Many U.S. intermediary organizations have ignored the most basic rules of development assistance concerning issues such as local presence, the design of technical assistance, local ownership of projects, local capacity-building, and sustainability. They have instead operated in a shallow, almost "fly by" manner in which assistance is parachuted into the recipient countries in occasional large loads and only superficially crafted to work in the local environment. This non-developmental approach has become somewhat less prevalent in the past several years as U.S. organizations have begun to learn from their mistakes and to take steps such as keeping local representatives in-country for longer periods, moving away from one-time conferences, and taking seriously the issue of local involvement. Nonetheless the fundamental problems largely remain.

Some of the shortcomings in the implementation of U.S. democracy assistance result from the fact that the entire aid structure for the region had to be assembled almost from scratch after 1989 and was put together in a tremendous hurry. Moreover, some of the U.S. intermediary organizations involved were new entities with no experience in political development assistance or, in fact, with any other kind of foreign assistance. The roots of the non-developmental approach, however, are deeper than just these contextual features of the assistance in Central and Eastern Europe.

Ever since the mid-1980s, when the U.S. government again began to involve itself significantly in democracy assistance, U.S. assistance providers have evidenced a distinct tendency to not draw upon the significant reservoirs of knowledge about development assistance that have been amassed in the fields of social and economic development since the 1950s. Americans involved in democracy promotion efforts show a persistent tendency to conceive of such aid as fundamentally different from other types of foreign assistance. They seem to see it as being largely a matter of exposing people in non-democratic societies to the right ideas and information, with the implicit notion that the actual processes of institutional and societal change will unfold naturally once the necessary transfer of information has taken place.

This conception does become blunted and ultimately contradicted by the realities of actually carrying out assistance projects, and U.S. assistance providers do begin to adjust accordingly. In Latin America, for example, where the U.S. government has been engaged in democracy assistance most extensively and for the longest period, a real evolution has occurred in the U.S. approach. The relatively shallow, non-developmental style of many of the democracy assistance projects of the 1980s has been replaced with a much more systematic, locally oriented, and long-term approach. The same evolution is slowly occurring with U.S. democracy assistance in Romania and probably in the rest of Central and Eastern

111

Europe as well, although the entire U.S. democracy promotion undertaking in the region seems more of a limited-term commitment than it does in other parts of the world.

AN ALTERNATIVE APPROACH

A fundamentally different approach to the implementation of democracy assistance in Romania has been taken by the Soros Foundations. The Soros Foundations are not organized along the lines of most other major Western private foundations engaged in international work. Instead of a single, central organization, they are a network of independent foundations primarily located in the recipient countries themselves. Two of the foundations, the Open Society Institute-New York and the Open Society Institute-Budapest, provide technical assistance and administrative support to the others. In Romania, the Soros Foundations operate through the Soros Foundation for an Open Society-Romania, a Romanian organization, with Romanian directors, management, and staff. Unlike any other major Western funding organization, Soros has created a structure that gives local persons nearly complete responsibility for the design and implementation of assistance programs.

The Soros approach also differs in the actual substance of the assistance programs. Soros programs make much less use than other Western programs of short-term visiting foreign experts. Instead, they emphasize supporting local sources of expertise and helping Romanians go abroad for short- to medium-term periods to develop their skills and knowledge. The combination of this emphasis and the locally run administrative setup means that a much higher percentage of Soros assistance is actually spent within Romania than is the case with most other Western assistance programs.

Another point of difference is that much of the Soros assistance in Romania takes the form of very small grants, ranging from $50 to $5,000. Soros-Romania has organized some large-scale projects, such as the provision of approximately $750,000 worth of newsprint to independent publications in 1992, but even such efforts tend to consist of a connected series of small- to medium-size grants. A further distinguishing feature is the high degree of transparency of the Soros operation. Competitions for Soros grants are openly advertised in Romanian newspapers, the names of the members of the selection committees are made public, and Soros-Romania produces an annual report, available in Romania, that lists every grant it makes.

In this study, which focuses on U.S. government assistance, I do not assess Soros-Romania's work. In the course of my research, however, I did interview a number of people who work or have worked with Soros-Romania, who have had contact with Soros as either grantees or applicants for funds, or who have observed Soros-Romania's operations. From these interviews and my own observations, I was struck by a number of very positive consequences of Soros-Romania's distinctive approach. The reliance on local staff and management has resulted in the training of a large number of talented Romanians in all aspects of administration, finance, and governance. The use of a large, well-supported local staff gives Soros-Romania a far deeper relationship to Romanian society than any other Western assistance provider. This results in programs reflecting a much greater understanding of local needs and mind- sets. The emphasis on small grants has also enabled Soros to reach many more people than any other assistance provider. The high degree of *local* transparency not only creates a local reputation for fairness but also has made Soros-Romania much better known in the country than other assistance providers such as USAID or the NED. Finally, the Soros concept of promoting societal openness as the central goal of its assistance is a very useful guiding idea. It projects a non-partisan, inclusive, and universal spirit that has helped to dispel the suspicions of many Romanians about a Soros operation in Romania (suspicions arising from George Soros's being of Hungarian and Jewish background and extremely wealthy) and to make the foundation accepted as a real national asset.

THE PRESSURE FOR RESULTS

During the first few years after 1989, not much attention was paid in Washington to the actual impact of U.S. efforts to promote democracy in Central and Eastern Europe. Those directly involved in the assistance programs were concentrating on getting them under way as rapidly as possible. Those who might be expected to sit in judgment of it, in the U.S. Congress and, more generally, in the policy community, the media, and the interested public—were still in an initial "wait and see" mode. In the past two or three years, however, this mode is steadily being replaced by a "prove it" attitude, as the total of U.S. assistance funds has grown large and the speed of overall political change in the region has slowed. The U.S. Congress, in particular, increasingly exerts pressure on U.S. donor organizations to demonstrate that spending millions of dollars on promoting democracy in Central and Eastern Europe is accomplishing something. This growing pressure is translated by the donor organizations, particularly USAID, into ever-rising demands on the recipients of their funds—both the U.S. intermediary organizations and local grantees—to produce frequent output reports and impact statements.

In Romania, those involved with U.S. democracy assistance are highly aware of this increasing pressure to show results. They acknowledge that the pressure has induced them to think more systematically and strategically about how to achieve their goals. They also concede that in the initial years after 1989, they tended to set goals that were far too ambitious, given the actual quantities of assistance being provided, and to craft only the vaguest of strategies for achieving the goals. Nonetheless they are adamant that the intense pressure to show rapid, measurable results is harmful in a number of ways.

To start with, the reductive nature of the reports that they are asked to make—the demand for vividly worded "bullets" encapsulating hard-hitting descriptions of successful project activities—leads them to emphasize the wrong aspects of their work. They might spend a month in small, low-key meetings in different areas of Romania building a consensus among a range of local actors to work together on a network for exchanging information. But if during that same month they instead organize a relatively perfunctory meeting with a group of MPs, that meeting will fit much more easily into the "output report" mold; they are therefore more likely to emphasize the meeting than the painstaking consensus-building. If they do hold a conference, they will feel a strong implicit pressure to report its most tangible, quantifiable features, such as the number of people who attend and the high-ranking status of some participants rather than its more subtle but ultimately more important features, such as which ideas did and did not attract attention at the conference and what new lines of communication among people or groups were established.

Furthermore, persons involved in the U.S. assistance work worry that the reporting distortions that result from the pressure to show quick, easily tangible results are beginning to have deleterious effects on the design of future projects. With the pressure to show results steadily intensifying, assistance projects are starting to be designed with an eye to what will produce good output reports and impact statements rather than what will actually advance civic education, human rights, judicial independence, or any other substantive goal. Projects are designed more to consist of highly visible public events than informal, fine-grained activity. And when public events are planned, the temptation increasingly is to make them large and to include at least some big names.

A related problem is that the heightened pressure to show results leads persons who are running projects purposely to misstate the actual results. Small successes are trumpeted as major breakthroughs. Minor, instructive failures are buried. Independent achievements by locals are rewritten as the fruits of assistance. Several past and present U.S. local representatives of democracy assistance projects told me that, in the face of what they believe to be unrealistic pressure to show a rich, steady stream of results from what are inevitably halting, difficult projects, they find themselves consistently overstating the results of their efforts. They do so not out of egotism or malicious intent but out of a desire to protect what they are convinced are valuable projects against a set of demands inimical to long-term, nuanced, low-profile democracy-building. And they strongly resent that they have to corrupt themselves in superficial ways in order to preserve their deeper sense of professional integrity.

Finally, the pressure for results has had unanticipated negative effects on Romanians involved with the U.S. assistance. Several Romanians who have worked on USAID-funded democracy projects mentioned to me that USAID does not seem to trust its contractors and grantees, since it is constantly asking them to report in excruciating detail on what they are doing. Worse yet, they said, USAID does not seem to trust itself, to have faith in its own democracy-building work. In their eyes, USAID sometimes appears to doubt whether its democracy assistance is of any value and needs the recipients of the assistance to keep telling USAID that it is. This apparently growing self-doubt, they say, which is so different from the robust sense of self-confidence about democracy promotion that Americans projected in the immediate aftermath of 1989, is inevitably transmitted to Romanians and is quite discouraging to them.

CONFLICTING PERCEPTIONS AND UNDERSTANDINGS
HISTORY EVER-PRESENT

Democracy assistance, like any type of foreign assistance, involves aid providers and local participants working in close, often sustained collaboration. Though they work together toward mutually agreed goals, the foreign providers and the local participants nonetheless often have conflicting perceptions and understandings about the assistance that joins them—an inevitable result of their differing roles in the relationship and their differing national backgrounds. In Romania, several areas of conflicting perceptions and understandings have surrounded U.S. democracy assistance. They are elaborated here both for their specific relevance to the Romanian assistance and as examples of the kinds of disjunctions that can arise with respect to democracy promotion anywhere.

One area of conflicting understandings concerns the general attitudes of aid providers and local participants toward the basic fact of U.S. democracy assistance. Most (though not all) Americans who went to Romania after 1989 to work on U.S. democracy assistance projects arrived in the country with a relatively simple, largely ahistorical set of ideas about their work. They tended to see the U.S. democracy assistance only in its immediate historical context—as one element of a general U.S. policy of supporting transitions to democracy and market economies in Central and Eastern Europe. To the extent that they put their work in a broader historical context, they conceived of the United States' post-1989 engagement in Eastern Europe as the final chapter of the successful U.S. Cold War effort to contain and indeed eliminate Soviet communism. Although they generally understood that the U.S. post-1989 assistance served U.S. economic and political interests, they also felt they were helping the recipient countries, and that the recipients of assistance should be grateful for this help.

The frame of reference for many Romanians who participated in or had contact with the U.S. assistance was very different. Many Romanians, especially those over forty years old, instinctively viewed the U.S. assistance, and Western assistance generally, as a new stage in the long, complicated historical relationship between Romania and "the West." This historical relationship is the source of much disappointment and bitterness to many Romanians, particularly as a result of what are commonly viewed in Romania as two major Western betrayals of Romania in the past fifty years: the "sellout" of Romania to the Russians by Roosevelt and Churchill at Yalta in February 1945 and the friendly relations extended to Ceauşescu by Western governments in the 1970s and 1980s in response to his foreign-policy independence from the Soviet Union. In the minds of many Romanians, these "betrayals" created a tremendous material and moral debt to Romania on the part of the United States and other Western countries. When Americans and other Westerners began hurrying to Romania after December 1989 to set up assistance projects, many Romanians interpreted this activity as the start of the much-delayed payback of this debt.

These very different American and Romanian frames of reference concerning the U.S. democracy assistance (and in fact all types of U.S. assistance) have led to misunderstandings. U.S. officials and Americans working for U.S. intermediary organizations in Romania tend to feel that, given the many pressures on the U.S. foreign aid budget and the lack of any strong Romanian-American constituency in the United States, the level of U.S. assistance to Romania is reasonably high. In contrast, many Romanians, at least those in Romanian political society, feel that the U.S. assistance has been much smaller than they expected—far short of the magnitude of the debt "owed" by the United States to Romania. They do not feel especially grateful for the U.S. assistance. For some, moreover, what they regard as the inadequate amount of U.S. assistance feeds an already ingrained bitterness about the West's neglect of Romania. Americans working on democracy assistance projects in Romania, in turn, are often surprised, and in some cases bewildered, by the complex emotions at play on the Romanian side, and they tend to underestimate the effects of those emotions on the overall progress of the assistance projects themselves.

PRINCIPLE VERSUS POWER

A related area of conflicting perceptions concerns the interpretation of U.S. democracy promotion efforts in terms of principle versus power. Most Americans involved in U.S. democracy assistance policies and programs in Romania tend to see such efforts as assertions of principle by the United States—the principle of supporting democratic transitions wherever they occur in the world. They expect Romanians to interpret these policies and programs as expressions of America's belief in democracy and its desire for other countries to benefit from democracy. At least some Romanians, however, interpret U.S. democracy promotion efforts in Romania first and foremost as an assertion of U.S. power—an expression of the vast imbalance between the United States and Romania in terms of political, military, and economic power.

Not surprisingly, this clash in perceptions arises most starkly when—in the name of democracy—the U.S. government presses

117

the Romanian government to accept something that it does not want to accept. For example, when the State Department as well as NDI pushed the Romanian government to permit domestic monitoring of the 1992 national elections, the Americans involved saw their efforts as the assertion of principle: the right of a people to free and fair elections. Romanian officials, who doubted the need for domestic observers and perceived the monitoring issue to be part of the opposition's partisan agenda, were somewhat cynical about America's self-proclaimed assertion of principle; they felt instead that they were confronting the naked fact of the United States' position as the dominant geopolitical power. The Americans involved thought that the Romanian government was acting in bad faith in resisting a valid expression of the principle of democracy; Romanian officials, for their part, felt the Americans were showing bad faith in cloaking an assertion of power in the misleading garb of principle.

IMPLEMENTATION AND IMPACT: INVERTED IMAGES

Further conflicting perceptions reside at the more specific level of the methods of implementation of assistance. Most U.S. organizations involved in democracy assistance in Romania, both donors and intermediary organizations, have the self-image of organizations that follow an operating method that is both transparent and procedurally fair. They regard transparency both as a necessary feature of politically sensitive assistance work and as a value that should be conveyed to Romanians to help begin to reverse the traditional secrecy of Romanian political and bureaucratic life. Similarly, they view procedural fairness as crucial to successful assistance work and as a value that should be propagated in Romania to counteract ingrained patterns of personalism and corruption.

Yet in talking with Romanians who have had direct or indirect contact with U.S. democracy assistance programs, I discovered that many Romanians do not see U.S. assistance organizations in these terms. They report great difficulty in obtaining precise information about U.S. organizations in Romania—what funding opportunities they offer, how Romanians should go about seeking assistance from a U.S. organization, and the like. It may be that such perceptions arise in part because of Romanians' own inhibitions and lack of experience in obtaining information of this sort. The point is the substantial gap in perceptions, whatever its cause.

And it does appear that the reporting of U.S. assistance organizations on their activities is directed much more to Washington audiences than to Romanians.

With respect to procedural fairness, several Romanians commented to me that they frequently hear Americans involved in assistance projects in Romania bemoan the personalistic style of Romanian political life and tout the American values of impartiality and fairness. Yet when it comes to giving out grants or choosing partners for technical assistance efforts, the same Americans will tell them to be sure to turn to them personally for help. And the decisions made by the U.S. organizations seem to Romanians to revolve around small circles of friends and contacts with whom the Americans are personally comfortable.

Finally, perceptions differ greatly between Americans and Romanians as to the relative impact of U.S. assistance efforts upon processes of change in Romania. As might be expected, Americans involved in the assistance projects tend to attribute much greater effects to the projects than do Romanians. Sometimes the difference is quite striking. For example, IRI staff members described to me intensive efforts on their part in the 1990-91 period to encourage the Romanian opposition parties to form a coalition. The formation of the Democratic Convention, one IRI representative told me, was "one of IRI's major accomplishments in Romania." Yet when I discussed the formation of the Convention with Romanian politicians who were directly involved, none of them mentioned an IRI role. When I asked them about IRI's role and mentioned IRI's own assessment of its role, they reacted with derision to the notion that IRI or any other foreign actor had any significant role in the intensive political negotiating among opposition leaders that led to the formation of the Convention.

The issue is not who was right about this point but the fact that such a marked difference exists in perceptions of the significance of assistance. I have here highlighted the example of IRI and the Democratic Convention, but the same pattern holds for most of the U.S. democracy assistance projects in Romania. It is scarcely a surprising pattern. Providers of assistance have a natural tendency to overestimate the importance of their work—both because they want to justify the assistance to their domestic audience and because they are so deeply engaged in the assistance that it inevitably seems central. Recipients have a matching natural inclination to downplay the effects of assistance (except when it comes time to make the case for getting more) out of a desire to feel that positive changes were the result of their own efforts. The gap in perception seems to be higher in the area of democracy assistance than in other areas of foreign assistance in Romania because of the greater intangibility or vagueness of the actual effects. The result is almost two separate psychological worlds concerning the assistance—that of the external actors and that of the domestic actors. In the former, the assistance appears large and omnipresent. In the latter, it is as if the telescope were turned around, making the assistance appear shrunken and hard to see at all.

COMPARING U.S. AND EUROPEAN ASSISTANCE

EUROPEAN MODELS

The United States certainly is not alone in attempting to promote democracy in Romania. The field is crowded with European actors, including the British, German, French, Dutch, Danish, Swedish, and Belgian governments, the European Union, and other European multilateral institutions and private European foundations. With a few exceptions (such as, for example, a small British Know How Fund project to train Romanian police), the European programs reach the same sectors and institutions as the U.S. programs: political parties, Parliament, the judiciary, unions, NGOs, the media, local governments, and others. However, just as U.S. programs tend to embody U.S. assumptions about how particular sectors or institutions should be structured, European programs reflect European assumptions about these same sectors and institutions. The result is that although the areas of U.S. and European democracy assistance are generally similar, the actual thrust of the programs is, at least sometimes, fairly different.

This is true, for example, with respect to assistance to support NGO development. In general, Western Europeans do not share the American fascination with NGOs and are much less prone to view NGO development as the crucial mechanism of democratic change. To the extent they do give attention to strengthening NGOs as a part of a political development agenda, they are less likely to emphasize policy-oriented NGOs, reflecting the fact that such organizations—and public-interest legislative advocacy as a strategy for achieving socio-political change—are less important in Western European countries than in the United States. Instead, they

120

tend to give equal or greater attention to social-service NGOs, arguing that it is just as important to foster local NGOs that solve everyday problems and are democratically run organizations as it is to build up high-visibility, public-interest NGOs, which have agendas that do not touch many individuals directly and often are internal autocracies.

Political party assistance is another area in which U.S. and European approaches differ. European political party assistance to Romania has been extensive. Political parties and party foundations in many European countries, including Great Britain, Germany, Belgium, Sweden, Holland, and Italy, give training and other support to fraternal parties in Romania. The Romanian Peasant Party has been the largest recipient of European assistance, attracting support from at least five different European parties. Unlike IRI's party work in Romania, which has been primarily aimed at the opposition coalition, the European political party programs are party-to-party—Christian Democrats assisting Christian Democrats (the Peasant Party), Social Democrats helping Social Democrats (the very small Romanian Social Democratic Party), and Liberals helping Liberals (the various Romanian Liberal parties). The European assistance is also on the whole less oriented than U.S. party assistance toward helping parties win particular elections and more aimed at studying the doctrines and platforms of the various parties—e.g., teaching Christian Democrats the principles of Christian Democratic ideology, Liberals about Liberal ideology, and so forth.

The differences in U.S. and European approaches to the method and content of party assistance reflect differences in underlying goals and assumptions. The U.S. party assistance is based on the "democrats vs. neo-communists" view of Romanian political life and seeks to strengthen the opposition relative to the governing parties. The European assistance is based on the view that Romanian political life is in an early, confused stage of development marked by a multiplicity of parties and ideological incoherence. The assistance aims to help clarify and establish the "normal" poles of democratic European political spectrums—Christian Democratic, Liberal, and Social Democratic—in Romanian political life.

JOINING EUROPE

The kinds of differences highlighted above between U.S. and European assistance programs relating to NGO development and political parties occur to a greater or lesser extent in all areas of democracy assistance. Underlying these differences is not only a basic division between American and European conceptions of the various institutional features of democracy, but also a fundamental difference between the American and European conception of the overall purpose of promoting democracy in Romania and in the region as a whole. For the U.S. donors and intermediary organizations, the effort to promote democracy in Romania is not just part of overall U.S. policy toward the region; it is an expression of a generalized U.S. impulse to assist democratic transitions wherever they occur. Many of these organizations tend to see the purpose of promoting democracy in Romania as helping that country join what many in the U.S. democracy assistance community refer to as "the international community of democratic nations."

In contrast, European democracy assistance efforts in Romania are in general much less rooted in a universalistic pro-democratic ambition than they are in a very specific regional agenda: helping Romania "join Europe." European democracy assistance is one element of a much broader European effort that aims to help bring Romania (and the other former communist countries of the region) into normative and institutional conformance with Europe on a whole range of political, economic, and social planes. This process reached its first major juncture in 1993, when Romania joined the Council of Europe, and looks ahead to the still very distant but no longer inconceivable goal of Romania's joining the European Union.

The different conceptual frameworks underlying the U.S. and European democracy assistance efforts contribute to a number of general differences in their overall design and implementation. The European assistance tends to be less partisan. It is not rooted in a lingering global anti-communist outlook that envisages a final victory by one set of political forces, but in a vague idea of gradual political normalization. This notion of political normalization points to a need to include all political actors in assistance programs, to bring the whole society along together. Unlike the U.S. assistance, the European assistance tends to assume a long-term process of external involvement rather than a short- to medium-term, intensive "turnaround" period of involvement. The European programs also aim to meet more explicitly defined criteria of success; the Council of Europe and other European multilateral institutions have set formal standards and norms for the political, legal, and economic realms that are both specific and far-reaching.

Highlighting these distinguishing features of European democracy assistance vis-à-vis U.S. democracy assistance is not meant to suggest that the European assistance is generally more effective than the U.S. assistance, but only to identify its different underlying frameworks and guiding assumptions. To the limited extent that I gained an impression of the actual functioning of European assistance programs, I found them to be afflicted with shortcomings of their own. One problem is that the European assistance efforts in the democracy or governance realm suffer even more than the U.S. programs from an over-reliance on conferences and seminars featuring visiting experts. Many European programs are highly academic in nature—a fact that aggravates many Romanian participants and causes them to point to the U.S. (and British) programs as more often having a higher practical content.

Another problem is that of arrogance. Although some Romanians complain about condescension on the part of Americans involved in promoting democracy in Romania, they reserve a special venom for what they see as the much more frequent, almost habitual arrogance of Western Europeans who come to Romania to work on democracy assistance programs. The condescension of Americans, Romanians say, is at worst a generalized sense of Romania as a disadvantaged country, a deprived child to be helped along; whereas the Western European attitude is a much more focused, historical contempt for the Balkans and all things "Eastern" in Europe. Finally, many of the European assistance programs, especially those of multilateral European institutions such as the European Union, seem to be hampered by bureaucratic rigidities as bad as or worse than those found in the U.S. programs.

DONOR COORDINATION

There is very little coordination of the democracy assistance activities of the many external actors in Romania. Political party assistance provides one example of this. The Peasant Party has been receiving support, mostly training, from parties in at least six different Western countries. These different foreign parties seem to be only dimly aware of each other's activities. When I asked one of the Peasant Party officials involved in these assistance relationships how the party tries to coordinate the aid it receives, he shrugged smilingly and said each foreign backer has its own relationship with particular party officials, rendering coordination impossible.

Policy coordination with European donors also seems to be lacking at the level of planning. A recent strategy statement produced by the USAID mission in Bucharest, for example, analyzes the ways U.S. assistance will affect the many different sectors it targets in Romania without once mentioning the existence of a wide range of European aid programs dealing with exactly the same sectors.[39] This strategy statement mentions no opportunities for building productively on non-U.S. assistance projects, contains no discussion of how local sectors or institutions receiving assistance from multiple sources might divide the field, and in general conveys absolutely no sense that Romania is highly penetrated by external assistance and that U.S. aid is only one relatively modest part of that overall picture.

The various Western aid organizations do sometimes hold coordination meetings in Bucharest. According to people who have attended such meetings, however, they are *pro forma* sessions of little utility. The donors share only superficial, formal information about their programs and do not actively explore possibilities for mutual cooperation and synergy. Given the self-enclosed nature of both bilateral and multilateral aid bureaucracies, it is unlikely that coordination can be significantly increased among the many external actors in Romania or other countries. The most useful approach to reducing duplication of efforts is for donors to try to be as open as possible in their activities and to insist on transparency on the part of recipient organizations with respect to what assistance they are receiving. Some Romanian NGOs have made progress in making available to potential donors the amounts and sources of their external funding. But much more remains to be done on this front in other sectors of democracy assistance, such as aid to political parties, trade unions, and the media.

CONCLUSIONS

Although the recent resurgence of U.S. democracy assistance is already more than ten years old, and well over a billion dollars has been spent on such programs around the world since the mid-1980s, very basic questions still surround the entire enterprise: What does such assistance actually accomplish? Does U.S. assistance utilize the right strategies and methods of implementation? What do the assistance recipients think of it? How should the assistance be evaluated? How do U.S. democracy assistance efforts relate to overall U.S. foreign policy? How do U.S. assistance programs compare to those of other actors, such as Western European countries and multilateral organizations?

It is worth pausing to consider why so many fundamental questions remain largely unanswered about a field of activity that is now so extensive and that has a history going back not just ten years, but decades, if one counts the previous waves of U.S. involvement in political development assistance. One reason is that the answers to most of these questions lie in the field, where the assistance is carried out—far from Washington, where the debates over assistance take place. It often seems that the debates in Washington about the value of U.S. democracy promotion efforts remain stuck at the level of general principles and deal too little with the specific realities of the assistance.

Another reason is that a deeply defensive culture has grown up around such assistance; the people directly involved in designing and implementing democracy promotion efforts—the very people who, along with the recipients, have the best perspective for understanding it—tend to become steadfast, even intransigent publicists for it. They gravitate toward a defensive mode in part as a reaction to the negative atmosphere that surrounds foreign aid generally in Washington, and to the sporadic but memorable (though often quite poorly informed) critical shots leveled at democracy assistance by the media. In addition, some of the persons involved in democracy assistance have an almost missionary attitude about their work that brooks no doubt.

The answers to the various outstanding questions about democracy assistance obviously vary from country to country and region to region. A single-country case study inevitably sheds only limited light beyond the boundaries of the particular country and region under examination. Nonetheless even some limited empirical grounding is useful as a start toward answering the broader questions. Moreover, the relatively centralized nature of the main U.S. aid providers, and the strong common framework of assumptions among them, leads to a certain sameness of assistance efforts across highly diverse recipient countries, rendering single-country findings more widely relevant than might initially be expected. I will not repeat here all of the specific findings discussed throughout this study, but will instead highlight some conclusions about three core issues: effects, strategy, and implementation.

The main point about effects is simply that we must bring our expectations about the impact of democracy assistance into line with the actual magnitude of our efforts. In rather grand fashion, the U.S. government in 1989-90 declared its intention to help the former communist countries of Central and Eastern Europe achieve transitions to democracy and capitalism. Since then, at least in the realm of democracy assistance, the United States has supplied a few million dollars of assistance per year per country in fulfillment of that intention. In Romania, the effects of this assistance have ranged from modest to negligible. The many training programs, technical assistance efforts, equipment donations, small institutional grants, and visitor exchanges have helped spread ideas about democratic practice in the emergent post-communist political society. But they have not dramatically reshaped institutions, changed power balances, or modified the basic political course of the society. The results are disappointing if measured against the expectation of a pivotal U.S. role, but they are in fact quite commensurate with the U.S. outlay.

U.S. democracy assistance in Romania has had greater positive effects when directed to people and organizations that clearly have their own internally generated impetus to engage in reform activities, such as the many civic activists who have made good use of their external assistance. It has had lesser positive effects when targeted at institutions or sectors that have shown little real commitment to reform, such as the judiciary and Parliament. To use a very simple analogy, it appears that democracy assistance works best as additional fuel in the tank of an already moving car; it cannot very easily fill an empty tank or serve as a replacement motor for a stalled vehicle. Faced with complex transitional societies presenting an array of diverse socio-political institutions and sectors, some evolving and some stagnant, assistance providers with limited budgets must target their aid at the areas where an impetus to reform exists rather than to where they think reform should exist. This does not mean that stagnant institutions must be completely written off—only that assistance must be more carefully directed to reform elements that can impinge positively on such institutions rather than force-fed to the institutions as a whole, in hopes of generating change.

A further point about the effects of democracy assistance is that the psychological, emotional, and moral impact of the assistance on individuals may be as or more important than the specifically intended "objective" effects on the shape and functioning of target institutions. Although U.S. democracy assistance has had at best modest effects on particular institutions in Romania, for a sizable number of people there, it has represented an important external validation of their striving to make Romania a democracy. Some Romanians also say that by participating in assistance programs, particularly those which involve long-term, collaborative relationships between U.S. assistance providers and Romanian organizations, they have gained fundamental knowledge about how a person thinks and acts in a democratic society—knowledge that has changed their basic outlook and behavior.

These relatively subjective and often highly individualized effects do not fit neatly into the reductionistic grids that U.S. assistance providers increasingly utilize to evaluate their programs. As a result, there is often a significant gap between how the effects of assistance are assessed in Washington and how they are felt and appreciated in the recipient countries. USAID and other U.S. assistance providers should be wary of trying to impose on democracy assistance programs pressure for short-term, quantifiable results. Such an optic not only misses important elements of what is actually being achieved by the assistance but also tends to distort and limit the evolutionary development of the assistance programs. Faced with expectations of rapid, measurable results, persons involved in assistance at the working level will end up designing and implementing programs just to produce those sorts of results—

no matter how artificial or mechanistic—instead of doing what is actually necessary to foster long-term, sustainable democratization.

As for the strategies underlying U.S. democracy assistance, the checklist approach that was hurriedly adopted in the aftermath of 1989 in Central and Eastern Europe—developing assistance programs to correspond to a fixed checklist of what are held to be the key institutional features of Western democracy—has outlived its short-term usefulness. It relies too much on particularly American models of specific institutions—models that are not necessarily well-suited to other societies, especially ones strongly influenced by continental European democratic models. More generally, in its strong emphasis on institutional endpoints, the checklist approach gives inadequate consideration to the socio-political processes and values underlying democratic development.

The partisan strategy that the United States has pursued in Romania (particularly in the initial years after 1989), and to a lesser extent in Bulgaria and Albania, is also seriously flawed. It is highly problematic when the United States uses assistance programs to favor one side of the political spectrum in societies which, even if not wholly democratic, are nevertheless pluralistic, with a wide range of established political parties and relatively open electoral competition. The positive effects of such an approach tend to be much weaker than anticipated. As U.S. assistance providers have discovered in Romania, transforming weak, disorganized opposition parties into a winning political force ("building an opposition," as U.S. officials confidently described their work in 1990 and 1991) is not easy. And significant unanticipated negative effects can occur—including fueling a siege mentality among the disfavored local political forces, giving a partisan hue to the other components of the U.S. democracy assistance effort, and heightening rather than reducing the unproductive divisiveness of local political life.

It was understandably appealing in 1990 to imagine that the United States could help complete the only partial anti-communist revolutions in the southern tier of the region by helping still-formative democratic forces drive the former communists out of power and off the political stage altogether. But by the mid-1990s, that ambition appears chimerical. It is apparent now that the path of democratization in these countries will not mean former communist political forces becoming extinct but, instead, gradual processes of evolution in which those forces learn to play by democratic rules and come to occupy a legitimate place in the democratic political spectrum. U.S. democracy assistance must adjust to this reality.

To reestablish a general strategic approach for democracy assistance around the region, U.S. assistance providers should back away from the institutional endpoints that make up the checklist approach and focus instead on a set of more general democratic values and processes, such as participation, representation, pluralism, and openness. Under such an approach, democracy assistance programs would aim to promote these values and processes on the assumption that democracy will progress in a given country not when the socio-political institutions take on certain pre-defined forms, but when participation, representation, pluralism, and openness increase. Such an approach cannot boast the definiteness that the checklist approach at least promises and that Americans want so badly. But it is better suited to the very modest amounts of assistance that the United States is actually providing, and it permits greater flexibility and local sensitivity with regard to actual programming.

If U.S. assistance providers wish to take a more pointed approach in countries with entrenched power structures of questionable democratic fidelity, they should avoid the partisan strategy of trying to help a certain part of the political spectrum gain power and should instead pursue a more general strategy of helping to decentralize power. Decentralization in such a context refers not simply to strengthening local government relative to the central government (although that may be one part of the effort) but to the broader process by which centers of power outside the control (other than normal legal control) of the state are gradually strengthened. Such centers include the full range of non-state actors common in established democratic societies: private businesses, independent media, political parties, religious institutions, labor unions, and the like.

A "decentralization of power" strategy may share with a partisan strategy a skepticism about the democratic intentions of the dominant political forces, but it differs from it in important ways. It does not focus on elections and on who holds the political reins of power but, rather, on the overall configuration of power within the society. It does not exclude certain political forces from the assistance programs but quite specifically seeks to open channels of communication between different sectors in order to reduce rather than heighten polarization. And it has little ideological content or objective beyond the very general notion that breaking up lingering statist power monopolies is essential to democratization in post-communist societies. A decentralization strategy emphasizes socio-political change at the local more than the national level, seeks useful ties between economic assistance and democracy assistance, and of course has much to do with civil society development, though not merely in the narrow sense of promoting policy-oriented NGOs.

The methods of implementing U.S. democracy assistance in the region also require revision. It is clearly time to move away from the non-developmental approach that has characterized such assistance since 1989. Heavy reliance on visiting U.S. experts, U.S. local representatives, short-term training, one-time conferences, and the like was probably inevitable in the initial period after 1989, when the U.S. assistance providers were trying to get assistance rapidly under way in countries with which they were largely unfamiliar. Six years down the road, however, such methods no longer have much place and are wearing badly in the recipient countries.

U.S. assistance providers, particularly USAID, need to work on getting a much higher proportion of their aid directly to people and organizations in the recipient countries. This does not mean that U.S. intermediary organizations should have no role at all, but that their role should be substantially modified from being lead organizations in assistance projects to being technical partners working in collaboration with local organizations. U.S. intermediary organizations need to give far greater attention to local-capacity building. Local people need to be brought much more into the process of designing and implementing assistance, making decisions about the specific allocation of funds, and shaping the delivery of technical assistance.

Such a shift in methods of implementation requires many specific operational changes. Above all, however, it requires some basic changes in attitude. In Romania, at least, U.S. officials have been very hesitant about giving U.S. assistance dollars directly to locals. It seems so much safer and easier to give funds to U.S. organizations. That inhibition must be overcome if the assistance is to improve. In addition, U.S. assistance providers must alter their overall conception of the implicit relationship in democracy assistance between the providing society and the recipient society. They must cease thinking of democracy assistance as a substance, like a spray, that the United States applies to other societies from a certain distance. They must see it instead as a series of occasions and relationships in which the United States and the recipient societies have an opportunity to work together side by side on issues of mutual interest and concern.

Such changes in attitude may seem too drastic or speculative to be realistic. But we must take note of the fact that a quite major concrete example of assistance being carried out in accordance with such ideas already is in place. In Romania and many other countries of the region, the Soros Foundations are operating with a highly localistic methodology and proving that although such a methodology is not a panacea, it can work very well.

I wish to close with a more general point. Ever since I began this study, people who have heard about it have pressed me for a summary judgment. "Well, what's the answer," they say, "is all this democracy stuff worthwhile?" Just sum it up, they implicitly or explicitly ask—yes or no? The desire for an objective, certain answer reflects the deep uncertainty many people have about a form of foreign assistance that is intuitively appealing but troublingly vague. The desire for a simple answer reflects the common, albeit unfortunate tendency in Washington to reduce debate over massively complex policy issues to arguments over bare, polarized alternatives, with the drive for simplicity running roughshod over any possibility of real understanding. I have generally disappointed people who have posed this question to me; I have pleaded complexity, not delivering a resounding yes or no.

What is difficult to explain is that the answer to the question of whether democracy assistance in Central and Eastern Europe is worthwhile depends a great deal on what we expect from such assistance and what we are willing to tolerate in its pursuit. It depends on whether we are willing to settle for only incremental, unquantifiable positive effects; to accept that the value of assistance may become clearly apparent only years from now; and to live with the significant uncertainties surrounding the whole enterprise of democratization and its promotion—recognizing that democratization can go badly awry, degenerating into conflict and violence, and that some of our interventions to promote democracy may not stop such outcomes and may even contribute to them. It is also not enough for the small world of assistance practitioners to answer affirmatively to these questions; they must be able to persuade politicians and the public to face and accept these limitations as well.

Whether democracy assistance in Central and Eastern Europe is worthwhile depends not only on our expectations about the assistance but also on our aspirations for ourselves in the world. It depends on how much we value making a contribution—one that is not decisive, yet is not insignificant—to the post-communist political transformation of Central and Eastern Europe. We may try to find an answer to that question in the moral realm. Or we may relate it to the more specific question of the U.S. role in post-Cold War Europe. Or we may view it as one small part of the basic choice facing the United States between a future international course of renewed engagement or semi-detachment. However we ground our inquiry, we cannot answer the basic question about the value of assistance until we answer basic questions about our own values.

I believe that the United States should, on altruistic grounds, provide assistance to these countries, which are emerging from a terrible period in their histories. I also think it is in the U.S. national interest, and Europe's interest, for the United States to maintain an active role in Europe, and that assistance to Central and Eastern Europe is a natural part of such a role. I am also certain that engagement is the best choice for our country's overall international direction in the coming years. And so, despite the serious limitations, uncertainties, and risks of democracy assistance, and despite the need for substantial improvement in how we go about the task, I think such assistance is worthwhile. Paradoxically enough, the case for democracy assistance, and in fact for foreign assistance generally, may at times depend less on the specific impact of the assistance on others than on what the assistance says and means about ourselves.

NOTES

[1]On the role of democracy promotion in the Reagan administration's policy toward Latin America, see Thomas Carothers, *In the Name of Democracy: U.S. Policy Toward Latin America in the Reagan Years* (Berkeley, CA: University of California, 1991). A very positive assessment of the Reagan administration's general approach to democracy promotion is given in Tony Smith, *America's Mission* (Princeton, NJ: Princeton University Press, 1994).

[2]Carothers, "Democracy Promotion Under Clinton," *The Washington Quarterly*, Vol. 18, No. 4, Autumn 1995, pp. 13-25.

[3]It is very difficult to arrive at hard figures for the amount of U.S. government funds devoted to democracy assistance. The budget category of "Building Democracy" in the Clinton administration's international affairs budget request, for example, includes as democracy support all assistance—whether economic, humanitarian, or political—to the former Soviet Union and Central and Eastern Europe. The range of $300 million to $500 million stated in the text was given to me by AID officials and includes only assistance projects with specific pro-democratic content (such as parliamentary assistance, judicial reform, elections, and the other areas of democracy assistance programming listed in the text), not economic and humanitarian assistance given to support democratizing governments.

[4]Kevin Quigley, "Philanthrophy's Role in Eastern Europe," *Orbis*, Vol. 37, Fall 1993, pp. 581-98.

[5]Larry Diamond, *Promoting Democracy in the 1990s: Actors and Instruments, Issues and Imperatives* (Washington, D.C.: Carnegie Commission on Preventing Deadly Conflict, 1995); Thomas Carothers, "Recent U.S. Experience with Democracy Promotion," *IDS Bulletin*, Vol. 26, No. 2, April 1995, pp. 62-69.

[6]*SEED Act Implementation Report: Fiscal Year 1994* (Washington, D.C.: U.S. Department of State, January 1995).

[7]The World Bank was active in Romania and other Eastern European countries during the communist years. Also, some private U.S. groups gave assistance to Romania as early as the inter-war period. See, for example, the analysis of the Rockefeller Foundation's public health assistance to Romania in the inter-war period in Maria Bucur, "From Private Philanthropy to Public Institutions: The Rockefeller Foundation and Public Health in Inter-War Romania," *Romanian Civilization*, Vol. IV, No. 2, Summer 1995, pp. 47-60.

⁸The literature on democratic transitions in Central and Eastern Europe is large and rapidly growing. Analysis of external efforts to promote democracy in the region, however, remains scarce. Available studies include Janine R. Wedel, "U.S. Aid to Central and Eastern Europe, 1990-1994: An Analysis of Aid Models and Responses," *East-Central European Economies in Transition*, Study Papers submitted to the Joint Economic Committee of the U.S. Congress (Washington, D.C.: Government Printing Office, November 1994) (very useful, but focused primarily on economic assistance); *Briefing on U.S. Assistance to Central and Eastern Europe and the NIS: An Assessment* (Washington, D.C.: Commission on Security and Cooperation in Europe, February 17, 1995); Geoffrey Pridham, et al., eds., *Building Democracy? The International Dimension of Democratisation in Eastern Europe* (London: St. Martin's Press, 1994); Daniel Siegel and Jenny Yancey, *The Rebirth of Civil Society: The Development the Nonprofit Sector in East Central Europe and the Role of Western Assistance* (New York: Rockefeller Brothers Fund, 1992). On the general problem of evaluating democracy assistance programs, see Stephen Golub, "Assessing and Enhancing the Impact of Democratic Development Projects: A Practitioner's Perspective," *Studies in Comparative International Development*, Vol. 28, No. 1, Spring 1993, pp. 54-70.

CHAPTER 2

⁹On the Ceauşescu era, see Vlad Georgescu, *The Romanians: A History* (Columbus, OH: Ohio State University Press, 1991), Chs. 6 and 7; Michael Shafir, *Romania: Politics, Economics and Society* (London: Francis Pinter Publishers, 1985); Daniel N. Nelson, *Romanian Politics in the Ceauşescu Era* (New York: Gordon and Breach, 1988); and Ion Mihai Pacepa, *Red Horizons* (Washington, D.C.: Regnery Gateway, 1987).

¹⁰Accounts and analyses of the events of December 1989 in Romania are numerous. See, for example, Matei Calinescu and Vladimir Tismaneanu, "The 1989 Revolution and Romania's Future," *Problems of Communism*, Jan.-April 1991, pp. 42-59; Martyn Rady, *Romania in Turmoil* (London: IB Tauris, 1992); Nestor Ratesh, *Romania: The Entangled Revolution* (New York, NY: Praeger, 1990); and Robert Cullen, "Report From Romania," *The New Yorker*, April 2, 1990, pp. 94-112.

¹¹The many articles on Romania by Dan Ionescu and Michael Shafir in *Report on Eastern Europe* and *RFE/RL Research Reports*, and now in *Transition*, provide much useful information and analysis of Romanian political and economic life since 1989. See also Thomas Gallagher, *Romania After Ceauşescu: The Politics of Intolerance* (Edinburgh: Edinburgh University Press, 1995); Vladimir Tismaneanu, "The Quasi-Revolution and Its Discontents: Emerging Political Pluralism in Post-Ceauşescu Romania," *East European Politics and Societies*, Vol. 7, No. 2, Spring 1993, pp. 309-48; Katherine Verdery and Gail Kligman, "Romania after Ceauşescu: Post-Communist Communism?," in Ivo Banac, ed., *Eastern European in Revolution* (Ithaca, NY: Cornell University Press, 1992); Liliana Mihut, "The Emergence of Political Pluralism in Romania," *Communist and Post-Communist Studies*, Vol. 27, No. 4, 1994, pp. 411-22; and Yves G. Van

Frausum, Ulrich Gehmann, and Jurgen Gross, "Market Economy and Economic Reform in Romania: Macroeconomic and Microeconomic Perspectives," *Europe-Asia Studies*, Vol. 46, No. 5, 1994, pp. 735-56.

[12]For an overview of U.S. relations with Ceauşescu, see Joseph Harrington and Bruce Courtney, *Tweaking the Nose of the Russians: Fifty Years of American-Romanian Relations, 1940-1990* (Boulder, CO: East European Monographs, 1991).

[13]Roger Kirk and Mircea Raceanu, *Romania versus the United States: Diplomacy of the Absurd, 1985-1989* (New York, NY: St. Martin's Press, 1994).

CHAPTER 3

[14]*The New York Times*, June 26, 1993.

[15]Joshua Muravchik, "U.S. Political Parties Abroad," *The Washington Quarterly*, Vol. 12, No. 3, Summer 1989, pp. 91-100.

[16]One analyst argues that the 1992 parliamentary elections were substantially distorted by fraud. See Henry F. Carey, "Irregularities or Rigging: The 1992 Romanian Parliamentary Elections," *East European Quarterly*, Vol. 29, No. 1, March 1995, pp. 43-66.

[17]*Chicago Tribune*, May 22, 1990.

[18]The IRI-NDI statement appears in the report jointly published by IRI and NDI in 1990 entitled *The May 1990 Elections in Romania*. The State Department statement is reproduced in *American Foreign Policy, 1990*, Document 169 (Washington, D.C.: Department of State, 1991), pp. 334-35.

[19]For a critique of the Law and Development Program, see James Gardner, *Legal Imperialism: American Lawyers and Foreign Aid in Latin America* (Madison, WI: University of Wisconsin Press, 1980).

[20]For example, CEELI's 1993 Annual Report states that "CEELI's work in Romania has focused primarily on strengthening and promoting an independent judiciary."

[21]José E. Alvarez, "Promoting the 'Rule of Law' in Latin America: Problems and Prospects," *George Washington Journal of International Law and Economy*, Vol. 25, 1991, pp. 281-321; Carothers, *In the Name of Democracy*, Ch. 6.

[22]*Weighing in on the Scales of Justice: Strategic Approaches for Donor-Supported Rule of Law Programs*, USAID Programs and Operations Assessment Report No. 7, February 1994.

[23]*Public Opinion Barometer*, The Institute for Quality of Life, Bucharest, September 1995, p. 28.

[24]In 1995, Frost Committee members met with members and staff of the Romanian Parliament to discuss the possible inclusion of Romania in the program.

[25]On the limited transparency of the Romanian Parliament, see Edwin Rekosh, ed., *In the Public Eye: Parliamentary Transparency in Europe*

and North America (Washington, D.C.: International Human Rights Law Group, 1995), Ch. 17.

[26]There is a burgeoning literature on the meaning of civil society. A few recent works include Ernest Gellner, *Conditions of Liberty: Civil Society and Its Rivals* (New York, NY: Allen Lane/Penguin Press, 1994); Adam Seligman, *The Idea of Civil Society* (Princeton, NJ: Princeton University Press, 1995); John Hall, ed., *Civil Society: Theory, History, Comparison* (Cambridge, U.K.: Polity Press, 1995); and Michael Walzer, ed., *Toward a Global Civil Society* (Providence, RI: Berghahn Books, 1995).

[27]Gordon White, "Civil Society, Democratization and Development (I): Clearing the Analytical Ground," *Democratization*, Vol. 1, No. 3, Autumn 1994, p. 379.

[28]One exception is the Soros Foundation in Romania, which has been trying to develop local corporate sponsorship for Romanian NGOs. In October 1995, for example, Soros sponsored a conference in Bucharest bringing together Romanian companies and Romanian NGOs to discuss NGO funding.

[29]Paul G. Buchanan, "The Impact of U.S. Labor," in Abraham F. Lowenthal, ed., *Exporting Democracy: The United States and Latin America* (Baltimore, MD: Johns Hopkins University Press, 1991).

[30]Larry S. Bush, "Collective Labor Disputes in Post-Ceauşescu Romania," *Cornell International Law Journal*, Vol. 26, No. 2, Spring 1993, pp. 373-420; Dan Ionescu, "Trade Unions in Romania Abandon Political Neutrality," *RFE/RL Research Report*, Vol. 1, No. 12, March 20, 1992, pp. 12-15; and Dan Ionescu, "Romania: Trade Unions a Growing Force," *Report on Eastern Europe*, March 29, 1991, pp. 38-45.

[31]A highly critical account of FTUI's work with *Frăţia* is set out in Eleanor Kennelly, "Labor After the Fall," *Insight*, July 12, 1992, pp. 7-13, 26-29.

[32]Ronald H. Linden, *The National Endowment for Democracy in Romania 1990-1992* (Washington, D.C.: The National Endowment for Democracy, January 1993), p. 14.

[33]A recent survey indicates that 38 percent of Romanians have satellite or cable service for their television. *Public Opinion Barometer*, The Institute for the Quality of Life, Bucharest, September 1995, p. 22.

[34]*Ibid.*, p. 25.

CHAPTER 4

[35]Alina Inayeh (Pro Democracy Association), "Letter to the Editor of Harper's Magazine," (unpublished, 1995).

[36]See for example, Joan Nelson, *Intricate Links: Democratization and Market Reforms in Latin America and Eastern Europe* (New Brunswick, NJ: Transaction Publishers, in cooperation with the Overseas Development Council, 1994).

[37]This intersection between economic and political goals of NGO development has been much explored in Latin America in recent years. See, for example, Charles Reilly, *New Paths to Democratic Development in Latin America: The Rise of NGO-Municipal Cooperation* (Boulder, CO: Lynne Rienner, 1995).

[38]See, for example, Fred Hiatt and Daniel Southerland, "Grass-Roots Aid Works Best in Russia," *The Washington Post*, February 12, 1995, p. A1; and "Contracting Problems, Management Woes Plague AID in the Ex-Communist Bloc," *Legal Times*, May 31, 1993, p. 1.

[39]*United States Seed Act Strategy Update for Romania 1994-1997*, Submitted by American Embassy, Bucharest, Approved June 18, 1994.

INDEX

International Republican Institute
(IRI), 18, 19, 34, 35, 68, 103-104
election monitoring efforts by, 20,
30, 31, 45-50
parliamentary work of, 21, 39, 58-
61
political party work of, 29, 31, 32-
33, 36, 37-44, 50, 60, 94, 100,
119, 121
Italy, 121

Know How Fund, British, 120

Latin America, 1, 6, 7, 36, 44, 64,
74, 111
Law and Development Program, U.S.,
52
League for the Defense of Human
Rights (LADO), 20, 46, 61, 67
Liberal Democratic Party of Japan,
35, 104
Liberal parties (Romania), 121
Liga Pro-Europa, 67
Local elections. *See* Elections of
February 1992 (Romania)
Local government assistance
generally, 3
in Romania, 22, 89, 105-106

Media (Romania), 13, 15, 81-87
newspapers, 12, 82-85
television, 13, 81-82, 83, 85-87
radio, 82, 83
Media assistance, 3, 80-81
in Eastern Europe, 83
in Romania, 18, 21, 22, 83-87, 89
Mihai Eminescu Trust, 19
Ministry of Justice (Romania), 54
Mitrea, Miron, 76, 77, 78
Most-favored-nation trade status
for Romania, 15, 26, 29, 31, 32

Năstase, Adrian, 49
National Bank of Romania, 14
National Democratic Institute for
International Affairs (NDI), 6, 18,
19, 34, 35, 36, 37, 68, 118
election monitoring efforts by, 20,
30, 31, 45-50
support for Pro Democracy
Association, 20, 21, 31, 46, 62,
67, 71-72
National Endowment for Democracy
(NED), 2, 3, 18, 19, 22, 113
establishment of, 2, 35

human rights projects, 67
media projects, 81, 83, 84
overall Romania portfolio, 23
trade union projects, 75, 78
National Forum Foundation, 18
National Liberal Party (Romania), 11,
20, 36, 38
initial contacts with IRI, 38
National Peasant Party (Romania), 11,
20, 36, 37, 39
European support for, 121, 123
initial contacts with IRI, 38
National Salvation Front (Romania),
29, 39
and the May 1990 elections, 12,
20
emergence of, 10-11, 36
splitting of, 13-14, 37
U.S. view of, 27-28
National Union Bloc (Romania), 77,
79
Nationalist parties, Romanian, 14, 37
NATO, 14, 32
Partnership for Peace program, 15,
32
Non-governmental organizations, 65,
70-71, 73
in Romania, 61-63, 66-74, 92-93,
96, 102, 107, 124
West European view of, 120-21
Northeastern University, 83

Opposition parties, Romanian, 14,
15, 16, 17, 37, 58
problems of, 39-42
U.S. support for, 20, 21, 29-30, 35-
44, 89, 119, 128
views of election observation, 49-
51
Organization of African Unity, 2
Organization of American States, 2
Organization for Security and
Cooperation in Europe, 2

Parliament, Romanian, 14, 58, 60, 90
assistance to, 21, 39, 58-64
transparency of, 61-62
Parliamentary assistance, 57, 63-64
in Romania, 21, 39, 58-64, 89, 91,
126
Party of Social Democracy in
Romania (PDSR), 16, 37, 49, 58,
60, 62, 76
and the 1992 national elections,

ACKNOWLEDGMENTS

This study was made possible by support from the Carnegie Endowment for International Peace and the German Marshall Fund of the United States. The views I express in this book are, however, entirely my own. I am especially indebted to Morton Abramowitz, President of the Carnegie Endowment, and Deborah Harding, formerly of the German Marshall Fund, for their interest and support.

I am deeply grateful to the many people in Romania and the United States whom I interviewed, sometimes several times, about U.S. assistance to Romania. All of the U.S. and Romanian organizations I contacted were open to my inquiries. I particularly thank Jerry Hyman and Kathryn Stratos of USAID for their openness and genuine interest in my work, even when we disagreed.

I thank Matthew Frumin, Larry Garber, Gail Kligman, Dan Nelson, Dan Petrescu, Kevin Quigley, Vladimir Tismaneanu, and Janine Wedel for their comments on drafts and/or other assistance. Many people at the Carnegie Endowment have been tremendously helpful—I owe much to Paul Balaran and Paula Newberg for intellectual and moral support; Valeriana Kallab and Lynne Davidson for editorial assistance; Maria Sherzad and Chris Bicknell for outstanding administrative assistance; and Tony Lucero, Amit Nigam, and Sheila Oh for research assistance. Jeff Pennington and Suzan Negip of the IREX Bucharest office provided crucial logistical help and a friendly place to hang my hat in Bucharest. I am also grateful to Suzan Negip and Sandra Calinescu for their invaluable language instruction.

Most of all, I thank Laura Bocalandro, who showed remarkably cheerful patience in the face of the field research trips, the inevitable authorial absorption in an extended written work, and the undoubtedly unsettling specter of a once-normal husband suddenly prone to wandering around the house at odd hours listening to Romanian language tapes on a Sony Walkman, muttering to himself unintelligibly.

ABOUT THE AUTHOR

Thomas Carothers, a senior associate at the Carnegie Endowment for International Peace, has worked on democracy assistance projects in many parts of the world for the U.S. Agency for International Development and various U.S. non-governmental organizations. He was previously an attorney at Arnold & Porter in Washington, D.C., and has served in the U.S. Department of State as a member of the Office of the Legal Adviser. He has also been an International Affairs Fellow of the Council on Foreign Relations and a Guest Scholar at the Woodrow Wilson International Center for Scholars. Educated at Harvard College, the London School of Economics, and Harvard Law School, he is the author of a previous book, *In the Name of Democracy: U.S. Policy Toward Latin America in the Reagan Years* (University of California, 1991) and numerous articles on democracy promotion and U.S. foreign policy.

THE CARNEGIE ENDOWMENT FOR INTERNATIONAL PEACE

The Carnegie Endowment for International Peace was established in 1910 in Washington, D.C., with a gift from Andrew Carnegie. As a tax-exempt operating (not grant-making) foundation, the Endowment conducts programs of research, discussion, publication, and education in international affairs and U.S. foreign policy. The Endowment publishes the quarterly magazine, *Foreign Policy*.

Carnegie's senior associates—whose backgrounds include government, journalism, law, academia, and public affairs—bring to their work substantial first-hand experience in foreign policy through writing, public and media appearances, study groups, and conferences. Carnegie associates seek to invigorate and extend both expert and public discussion on a wide range of international issues, including worldwide migration, nuclear nonproliferation, regional conflicts, multilateralism, democracy-building, and the use of force. The Endowment also engages in and encourages projects designed to foster innovative contributions in international affairs.

In 1993, the Carnegie Endowment committed its resources to the establishment of a public policy research center in Moscow designed to promote intellectual collaboration among scholars and specialists in the United States, Russia, and other post-Soviet states. Together with the Endowment's associates in Washington, the center's staff of Russian and American specialists conduct programs on a broad range of major policy issues ranging from economic reform to civil-military relations. The Carnegie Moscow Center holds seminars, workshops, and study groups at which international participants from academia, government, journalism, the private sector, and nongovernmental institutions gather to exchange views. It also provides a forum for prominent international figures to present their views to informed Moscow audiences. Associates of the center also host seminars in Kiev on an equally broad set of topics.

The Endowment normally does not take institutional positions on public policy issues. It supports its activities principally from its own resources, supplemented by nongovernmental, philanthropic grants.

Carnegie Endowment for International Peace
2400 N Street, N.W.,
Washington, D.C. 20037
Tel.: (202) 862-7900
Fax: (202) 862-2610
e-mail: ceip@igc.apc.org

Carnegie Moscow Center
Mosenka Plaza
24/27 Sadovaya-Samotechnaya
103051 Moscow, Russia
Tel: (7-095) 258-5025
Fax: (7-095) 258-5020
e-mail: carnegie@glas.apc.org.

EUROPE IN THE BALANCE
SECURING THE PEACE WON IN THE COLD WAR
CHRISTOPH BERTRAM

This study masterfully brings into focus all of the separately debated issues that must be addressed together to secure the peace that was won in the Cold War: NATO

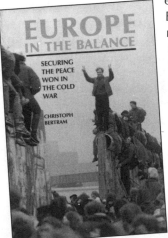

enlargement, challenges to cohesion within the European Union, the strength of the U.S.–Europe connection, reform and stability in Eastern Europe, and Russia's role in Europe. The study argues that Europe is the defining region where the elements of any new international order are being shaped; the next few years will determine whether Europe will find a new stability or fall back into old rivalries and tensions.

Christoph Bertram, formerly director of the International Institute for Strategic Studies in London and a senior associate of the Carnegie Endowment, is diplomatic correspondent for the German weekly, *Die Zeit*.

ISBN: 0-87003-068-X   **$12.95**

"Christoph Bertram's *Europe in the Balance* provides an admirable exploration of the dilemmas that bedevil Europe and the United States in trying to imagine and foster some new set of institutional arrangements to promote stability, democracy, and prosperity in the new European scene. . . . The book is an important contribution to a discussion whose results will weigh heavily on the future, here as well as in Europe."
—David P. Calleo
Dean Acheson Professor and Director of European Studies
School of Advanced International Studies
The Johns Hopkins University

"In this thoughtful and comprehensive attempt to rethink the tasks and structures of the Atlantic society of states after the Cold War, Christoph Bertram centers his analysis on an expanded NATO and an enlarged European Union, but he also proposes new institutions, both among the Atlantic states and between NATO and Russia. A sharp analytic realism and a plea for innovation and creativity are in constant tension—a tension which makes this essay both challenging and challengeable."
—Stanley Hoffmann
Douglas Dillon Professor of the Civilization of France
Center for European Studies, Harvard University

To order, call Carnegie's distributor, The Brookings Institution, toll-free 1-800-275-1447 or 202-797-6258. Fax: 202-797-6004. When ordering, please refer to code RVCC.

A CARNEGIE ENDOWMENT BOOK

TRACKING NUCLEAR PROLIFERATION
A GUIDE IN MAPS AND CHARTS, 1995

Leonard S. Spector and Mark McDonough with Evan S. Medeiros

Tracking Nuclear Proliferation provides specialists and the public alike with the latest available facts about the threat that Americans identify as their greatest foreign policy concern.

On the nature of the nuclear proliferation danger has changed dramatically in recent years. On the positive side, more nations than ever before are renouncing nuclear arms under strict international control—in some cases shutting down secret nuclear weapons programs and even giving up complete nuclear arsenals.

On the negative side, however, a handful of states continue to challenge international norms. Some are attempting to defeat the nuclear restraints they have accepted. Others, already undeclared nuclear powers, continue to enhance their nuclear forces. Equally threatening is the prospect of an international black market in nuclear goods. With the breakup of the Soviet Union and possible political instability looming in China, this danger is more serious than ever before. The first cases of smuggled weapons-grade nuclear material have already been documented.

To keep pace with these events, *Tracking Nuclear Proliferation* provides a comprehensive, country-by-country guide to the spread of nuclear arms in the mid-1990s. The present survey is the sixth in the Carnegie Endowment's series on proliferation prepared under the direction of Leonard S. Spector.

This 1995 assessment offers detailed information on key recent developments in a new, easy to use format featuring explanatory maps, charts describing the national nuclear programs of seventeen countries, and appendices introducing newcomers to the basics of nuclear technology and multilateral nuclear controls.

ISBN: 0-87003-066-3
Price: $12.95

To order, call Carnegie's distributor, The Brookings Institution, toll-free 1-800-275-1447 or 202-797-6258. Fax: 202-797-6004. When ordering, please refer to code RVCC.

A NEW CARNEGIE ENDOWMENT SERIES ON
INTERNATIONAL MIGRATION ISSUES

To contribute constructively to the policy debate on immigration in the United States and abroad—and to help deepen policymaker and public understanding of the migration and refugee situation worldwide—the International Migration Policy Program of the Carnegie Endowment for International Peace announces a new series of policy papers.

Three policy papers, listed below, are now available. Future issues focus on how the United States should select skilled immigrants; migration policy issues in Australia, Canada, Germany, and Japan; progress toward freedom of movement within the European Union; and the sources of modern conceptions of democratic citizenship.

1. MANAGING UNCERTAINTY:
Regulating Immigration Flows in Advanced Industrial Countries

Demetrios G. Papademetriou and Kimberly Hamilton identify and analyze the conceptual problems and principal issues involved in thinking about and developing contemporary immigration policy regimes. They argue that policymakers must develop immigration policies that are at once effective in dealing with changing world conditions, capable of reaping immigration's benefits, able to sustain public support, and consistent with international commitments.

ISBN 0-87003-069-8   Price: $ 5.95

2. U.S. REFUGEE POLICY:
Dilemmas and Directions

Kathleen Newland reviews four major elements of the U.S. refugee program—resettlement, temporary protection, first asylum, and emergency response—and argues that, as practiced, these do not add up to a coherent refugee *policy*. Minimizing the need for refugee protection should be the central thrust of post-Cold War U.S. refugee policy. Nonetheless, the difficulty of preventing or resolving refugee-producing conflicts means that robust U.S. leadership in providing protection is still urgently needed.

ISBN 0-87003-071-x   Price: $ 5.95

3. CONVERGING PATHS TO RESTRICTION:
French, Italian, and British Responses to Immigration

In this study, Demetrios G. Papademetriou and Kimberly Hamilton, focus on how France, Italy, and the United Kingdom are responding to the complex issues raised by immigration and asylum matters. They explore the often trial-and-error character of governmental responses to these issues, the absence of mainstream political-party leadership, and the growing disjuncture between initiatives motivated by increasingly restrictionist impulses and practical efforts to further the immigrant integration at the local level.

ISBN 0-87003-073-6   Price: $6.95

To order, call Carnegie's distributor, The Brookings Institution, toll-free 1-800-275-1447 or 202-797-6258. Fax: 202-797-6004. When ordering, please refer to code RVCC.

A CARNEGIE ENDOWMENT BOOK

UN PEACEKEEPING
JAPANESE AND AMERICAN PERSPECTIVES
Edited by Selig S. Harrison and Masashi Nishihara

For the past four decades, the United Nations has played a significant peacekeeping role based on the consent of the warring parties in Cyprus, the Golan Heights, the Congo, and other flashpoints of conflict. But the UN role in maintaining world order has been redefined and broadened in recent years to embrace peace enforcement efforts with or without the consent of the antagonists, often in combination with traditional peacekeeping.

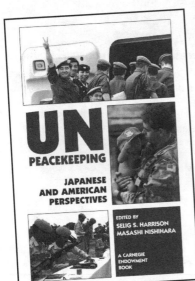

This dramatic change has provoked growing controversy both in the United States, hitherto the largest financial supporter of UN peacekeeping, and in Japan, where advocates of a larger Japanese global role are promoting expanded Japanese participation in UN peacekeeping missions.

UN Peacekeeping: Japanese and American Perspectives is the product of a research project co-sponsored by the Carnegie Endowment for International Peace in Washington and the Research Institute for Peace and Security in Tokyo. Eight American and Japanese specialists present contrasting perspectives on such issues as: (1) the criteria that should govern UN intervention in future conflicts; (2) the desirability and feasibility of combining peacekeeping and peace enforcement; (3) the limitations imposed by international law on UN intervention; (4) the record of UN intervention in key arenas of conflict, including Cambodia, where Japan has played a major role; (5) domestic attitudes toward UN peacekeeping in both countries; and the potential for Japanese-American cooperation in UN peace-making, peacekeeping, and peace enforcement.

Selig S. Harrison directs the Carnegie Endowment Program on Japan's Role in International Security Affairs. A former Northeast Asia Bureau Chief of *The Washington Post*, he is the author of five books on Asia.

Masashi Nishihara is Director, First Research Department, National Institute for Defense Studies, Tokyo, and Professor of International Relations, National Defense Academy, Yokosuka.

ISBN: 0-87003-066-3   **Price: $12.95**

To order, call Carnegie's distributor, The Brookings Institution, toll-free 1-800-275-1447 or 202-797-6258. Fax: 202-797-6004. When ordering, please refer to code RVCC.

THE NEW TUG-OF-WAR

Congress, the Executive Branch, and National Security

Jeremy D. Rosner

Since the birth of the Republic, U.S. foreign policy has been an uneasy joint venture between the executive branch and Congress. Now that the end of the Cold War has transformed world affairs and the 1994 elections have turned Capitol Hill upside down, how is Congress's role changing? As the United States faces an array of global challenges—from ethnic conflict to proliferation to trade—is congressional assertiveness in foreign policy a post-Vietnam relic or a post-Cold War inevitability? Is Congress pushing the United States toward isolationism or simply toward more selective internationalism?

The New Tug-of-War addresses these important questions, offering one of the first examinations of the post-Cold War relationship on national security between the White House and Congress. Jeremy Rosner analyzes the sources of change in the relationship—shifting definitions of security, lingering budget deficits, an influx of new members in Congress, partisan turnover in both branches—and traces their influence through detailed case studies of the work of the two branches on aid to the former Soviet Union and multilateral peacekeeping. The study highlights the potential and pitfalls for the executive-congressional relationship in a new security era.

Jeremy D. Rosner is a Senior Associate at the Carnegie Endowment for International Peace. From 1993 to 1994, he was a Special Assistant to President Clinton, serving as Counselor and Senior Director for Legislative Affairs on the staff of the National Security Council.

"Intellectually rigorous, politically savvy, substantively solid, and clearly written, Jeremy Rosner's The New Tug-of-War untangles the unpredictable, unexpected, and complex changes in the relationship between the presidency and Congress that have been triggered by the end of the Cold War. Scholars, journalists, and policy makers should read it for its insights—and heed its recommendations for the future."

—Norman J. Ornstein, American Enterprise Institute

"Rosner provides a first-rate analysis of a very timely issue: the changing nature of executive-legislative relations in foreign affairs.."

—James M. Lindsay, University of Iowa

ISBN: 0-87003-062-0   Price: $10.95

To order, call Carnegie's distributor, The Brookings Institution, toll-free 1-800-275-1447 or 202-797-6258. Fax: 202-797-6004. When ordering, please refer to code RVCC.